MW01601795

Labor of Love
A Mountain Teacher's Story

Daisy Copeland Jarrell

McClain Printing Company
Parsons, WV
www.mcclainprinting.com
2004

International Standard Book Number 0-87012-713-6
Library of Congress Control Number 2004091995
Printed in the United States of America
Copyright © 2004 by Daisy Copeland Jarrell
Polk City, FL
All Rights Reserved
2004

Foreword

For years, our mother, Daisy Copeland Jarrell, taught us through her example of Godly living, and through her life experiences. Most of the lessons we learned from her as children were centered on the lessons of her life. We became concerned that we might lose some of the richness of her story as she began to lose her eyesight and hearing. This prompted us to attempt to put some of her words in print so they could be passed on to future generations.

We attempted to capture her memories as accurately as possible, and in her own words. This was somewhat difficult because at age ninety-five she was nearly blind and deaf. Therefore her editorial skills were but a minuscule fraction of what they once were. Except for inaccuracies that may creep in because of these "impairments of age", these are her words as she told us. She started out being the author, and we are merely transcribers.

Unfortunately on April 24, 2002, Mom went home to be with her Savior, thus leaving this minor work largely unfinished. Because she liked the idea of documenting her life, we decided to put our collective heads together and finish it as Mom would have wanted. Now there is a minor problem with our memories being different, and no one with final authority. Chapters two through six were dictated and approved by her with only minor editing, after her death. Her children largely wrote other chapters, with considerable early guidance from her and reference to her journal.

Where there are differences in how we collectively remember things, we don't hide them, but try to give both sides, and sometimes, multiple sides. However, we think that in matters of consequence, we have captured the rich flavor of her life.

We are her children, Phyllis Jarrell Aquino, Donald Jarrell, Betty Jarrell Pennington, Billie Jarrell Bailey, Jerry Jarrell, and Garnet Jarrell Given.

Chapter One
Historical and Geographical Setting

It will be helpful in understanding the first section of the book to provide a brief description of the area where Mom spent these early years. This may be especially useful to those readers without prior knowledge of the place and time.

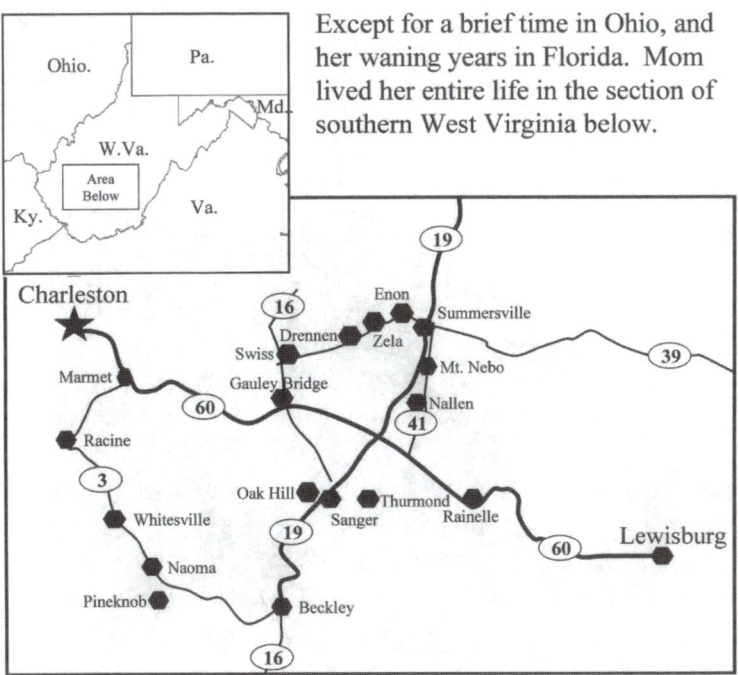

Except for a brief time in Ohio, and her waning years in Florida. Mom lived her entire life in the section of southern West Virginia below.

Although Mom's family frequently moved, with one exception (the few months spent in Norwalk, Ohio) they never moved far from Mom's birthplace. Place a 20-mile-diameter circle with its outside edges touching Swiss on the north, and Sanger on the south, and it will contain almost all the communities she mentions in the section of the book we have labeled "The Early Years." Yet, transportation in the area at that time, was such that even a short move could be surprisingly divisive for the extended family. For example, when Mom's family lived in Swiss, Nicholas County, and wanted to visit her mother's parents in Sanger, Fayette County, this 20-mile (as the crow flies) trip required about 45 miles of travel on the railroad, a change of trains at Gauley Junction, and a minimum of one and one-half hours on the train. If the train was not available, as when the family lived at Enon and Mom was teaching at Swiss, the approximately 25 miles was too far for her to commute or even to visit home except on holidays. In order to be near enough to Summersville to allow the children to walk to high school, the family had deliberately chosen for the first time to move beyond the reach of the railroad (which ran from Charleston through Swiss to Zela).

The nomadic nature of the family appears to have been largely due to the industry in which Grandpa chose to work. While he secured jobs in coal mining, small business, farming, or even manufacturing when necessary, his primary employment was in timbering. Of these industries, timbering required the most mobile workforce. Timber companies tended to harvest the better trees and then move to a new location of virgin timber. Employee housing was necessarily temporary in nature, either hastily built company-housing or rental housing. This, in turn, meant that it was relatively easy to move even when the move was not dictated by a need to relocate with the work.

Not only did the industry dictate and enable frequent moves of its employees, but it also required that they reside near rivers or large streams and railroads. Timber companies stayed close to the rivers and railroads of the area, since these provided their means of transportation. An ideal location was one near both a large stream and a railroad.

4

Since railroads were built along streams to take advantage of the gradual gradients, staying close to both at the same time often was possible. For example, the Gauley River, on which Swiss was located, was used to transport large numbers of cross-ties and log timber on rafts to saw mills. Most streams of any size were used to transport timber in this fashion.

Extensive railroad construction had occurred in the area during the last half of the19th century, and continuing into the 20th in order to obtain coal. The area had main line railroads traversing all the major streams (the Kanawha, New, Gauley, and Meadow rivers) with branch lines along the tributaries of the major streams. Two of the more important freight-carrying trains in this immediate area were the Chesapeake and Ohio and the Norfolk Southern. The C&O ran from Clifton Forge, Virginia, to Cincinnati, Ohio, with stations at Gauley Junction and Thurmond. A second train, that later was called the Norfolk Southern, ran from Zela through Gauley Junction to Charleston and Huntington and continuing into Ohio. (These two railroads also ran passenger trains that were frequently used by the family as, for example, on trips between Sanger and Swiss.) Sidings were constructed along the railroad tracks and empty timber cars ("empties") were left on these sidings by the railroads for loading and later delivery to the sawmill. Many of the logs were delivered to large band mills (saw mills which employed steam-driven band saws) that were located on major streams, and thus were positioned to make use of both river and train transportation. The most important band mills in this area were on the Meadow River and its tributaries at Nallen, Honeydew, and Rainelle. These mills were served by the Sewell Valley Railroad.

A final point to be made about this area is that the economy was, relatively speaking, quite good throughout the time span covered by the Early Years. In 1869, when Mr. J. G. Hurt, one of the original settlers of Sanger, first moved onto the property later known as "The Hurt Farm", the area was described as a grazing area whose citizens carried on an extensive business of raising and trading in livestock. It also was noted for its large beds of all kinds of coal and its primeval forests of superior timber. The Early Years were a period characterized by exploitation of these resources against a background of vibrant agriculture.

Industrialization created a heavy demand for coal, and Fayette County, as part of the Appalachian Basin, was a major supplier of this need. The state's coal production peaked in 1918, a level not to be attained again until 1947. In addition, there was a voracious demand for lumber to build cities and towns throughout the eastern United States. The lake states of Michigan, Wisconsin, and Minnesota, before 1900 the major suppliers of the nation's lumber, had been over-logged and lumber production in these states dropped off sharply after 1900. Peak harvesting of West Virginia's forests came in 1909. This area of Nicholas and Fayette counties, with its railroads and its abundant re-sources of coal and timber was well-positioned to take advantage of the new market opportunities. In fact, in some years during this period, more freight passed through Thurmond than through any other freight yard in the United States. (Unfortunately, over-rapid exploitation of the forests during this period led to forest fires and severe erosion during the 1920s and '30s.)

Chapter Two
The Early Years

For the record, I am Daisy Dell Copeland Jarrell, a retired schoolteacher with 46-years service, mother of six, grandmother of 21, and great-grandmother of 30.

My life began in West Virginia at a little place named Sanger in Fayette County. I often wondered if Mom knew she was going to give birth to identical twins, or if she was surprised when we arrived on July 9, 1906. There was no ultrasound to determine number or gender as there is today. Some of the time women didn't even see a doctor until the time of delivery, and in some cases, not even then. Often neighbor women helped each other with the birthing of their children, and sometimes midwives came to aid in the deliveries. I don't know who helped in our being born, but I recall Mom saying it was a very normal delivery. Even though she only carried us seven months, we were good-sized babies. I weighed five pounds and my twin weighed four pounds twelve ounces. We were welcomed into the family by an older sister, Bertha Ellen, who had been born on June 18th 1904.

Three weeks after we were born, my twin sister died. The cause of death was probably crib death, since she seemed quite healthy, and Mom found her dead in bed. She and I were in bed with Mom, as was the practice then for infants to sleep with their mother making it easier for the mother to breast feed, without having to get up at night. Mom felt for a long time that maybe she had smothered the baby in her sleep. We had not been named and when I was a little older, the others used to tease me and say maybe it was Daisy who died and I would get upset when they said that. When she died, they buried her in a christening gown Mom had made of a beautiful, soft white material with a full skirt gathered into a yoke overlaid with lace in front. It was very fancy, and I know it took some time to make. Mom had made one just like it for me. This is evidence Mom must have known she was carrying twins, because she had made two christening gowns. I still have a very vivid picture of my gown. Mom gave it to me when I was grown, but it was destroyed in a fire when the first house Don and I owned burned to the ground. There is a small stone marker in the Copeland Cemetery on Belle Creek at Marting, West Virginia bearing the inscription "INFANT; L. L. Copeland; July 9, 1906; August 2, 1906" which identifies her grave.

Shortly after our birth, and the death and burial of my twin sister, we moved to Newark, Ohio, for a brief time where Pop worked in a foundry making stoves.

We left Newark, and moved to Swiss in Nicholas County West Virginia where Pop worked as a log scaler for Flynn Lumber Company. A scaler measures logs to estimate how many board feet of lumber they will produce. Scaling was done on a moving train or in holding ponds, and a great deal of risk was involved as the scaler walked the logs scaling them on the moving cars, or floating in ponds. Often the logs would be covered with ice or snow, escalating the hazard. My grandfather, Winfield Copeland, worked as a lumber grader in the lumber mill. A grader's job was to value the lumber as to type and quality. Certain types of trees, hardwoods for example, produced lumber that was more valuable at the mill. Pop's sister Lettie's husband, Henry Gross, was an engineer on the log train.

Photograph 1 **This is a Flynn Lumber Company train as it pulled through Drennen to take its load of logs to the mill at Swiss. Pictured in the cab of the Climax locomotive are Engineer Henry Gross, and Fireman Mark Turner. Standing on the engine's front end are Jack Drennen and Dayton Ford.**

While we were at Swiss, Mom gave birth to Vernice DeLora on March 26, 1908. Her claim to fame, in her own words, was her unusually large birth weight. She weighed in at 16 pounds, and despite her weight, the company doctor delivered her at home with no great difficulty. Consider that her weight was 50% more than the combined weight of the twins at birth.

We lived in a company owned house, and like most of the company houses, it was crudely built with tar-paper on the outside to cover the huge cracks between boards that seasoned after being nailed on. Without the tarpaper, bugs, other critters, and the cold would have readily come through. Since wallpaper cost too much for a temporary house, the women papered the inside walls with newspaper. We learned to spell and read from these newspapers on the walls of company houses.

The next move was to a privately owned house at Swiss, known locally as the Belcher place. This was not a company house, and in that respect was unusual for us. For the first time, Mom had room for pigs, chickens, and a garden. These helped feed the family, which grew soon after we moved into the Belcher place. Garland Winfield was born on November 19, 1909 and weighed 12 pounds. Garland Winfield, the first boy of the family, and named for both grandfathers, was the pride of the family. Mom also had an extra room which was rented to travelers. Once I overheard one of the roomers snoring so loudly that I thought a cow was in the house. I woke Pop to get the cow out of the house. Pop immediately recognized the source of the "cow" noise.

Bertha contracted whooping cough her first term at school and it took a turn with each of us. Pop and Mom worked day and night nursing us, but unfortunately, after so many hours without sleep, they apparently failed to awaken when Garland had a coughing spell. Mom had fallen asleep with Garland in her arms, and awoke in the early morning to realize his weight felt different. She said she knew immediately he was dead, and yelled to Pop to bring a light. The light showed what she feared most, and already knew in her heart. Bert had a hard time handling this, as she felt she was to blame for bringing the disease home. Garland was buried at the Copeland cemetery where his grave is identified by a small marker.

Many years later, after Mom had died, Vernice found this poem among some papers in Mom's Bible. She had written "Our Darling Son" on it.

The angels came to our home one day
And carried our darling son far away.
The room was little and dark and small,
And I did not know they were there at all.
I had caught not the rustle of a wing.
I had heard not even an angel sing,
But swiftly and silently as the dawn
They came and took him, and he was gone

On September 22, 1911, Rita Faye joined our family at the Belcher place, and was the first "black-eyed" baby in the family. The summer before Faye was born Bertha had contracted diphtheria. Mom and Pop had taken us to visit Uncle Cal and Aunt Sarah whose baby girl, Garnet, had just died from what doctors had diagnosed as croup. Bertha soon became ill, and when the community erupted into a same-symptom epidemic, the doctor correctly diagnosed it as diphtheria. Vernice and I were inoculated and we escaped the illness, but Bertha almost died. They did the inoculation while we were asleep, and I couldn't believe they had done it and I had slept through it. Finally I felt a little piece of plaster on my backside, and was semi-persuaded that indeed I had received the shot.

We all got measles shortly after that and with Bertha's weakened condition, she was much more severely hit than the rest of us. She was left with a, later diagnosed, slight lameness in her right foot.

The Baptist church at Swiss was too far for us kids to walk, so we went regularly to a Sunday school held over a large hall in town. They gave us cards with a picture on one side and a corresponding Bible story on the back. The pictures, as I recall, were reproductions of classical paintings of biblical scenes. Mom and Pop didn't go to church with us

11

until a few years later. Pop was not living as he felt he should and Mom always had a small baby. Mom taught us about God at home, and we learned many hymns from hearing her sing them as she worked. Grandpa Copeland lived with Aunt Lettie at Swiss, and many pleasant Sunday afternoons were spent listening to him and Pop talking together, as he visited us nearly every Sunday.

Photograph 2 The Copeland family after Faye was born. (L-R) Me, Pop holding Faye, Bertha, Mom and Vernice.

Chapter Three
The Family Roots

Pop and Mom were Winfield Luther Lowell and Nannie
Hurt Copeland. They met in the Fall of 1902 at the home
of Pop's uncle, Dave Copeland, in Marting, a small mining
town in West Virginia. They were both boarding at Uncle
Dave's; Mom, so she could work her first and only term as
a school teacher; Pop, so he could work in the coal mines at
Marting. They were married the following year on September 6, 1903, at the farm home of Mom's parents, John
Garland and Bettie Ruth Field Hurt at Sanger, West Virginia. The Rev. J. B. Chambers officiated at the Sunday-
morning wedding in the presence of a few relatives: Mom's
parents and her maiden aunt, Mary Ann Fields, who lived
with them; her brothers. John Calvin and Jubal Edwin Hurt;
Calvin's wife Sarah, and their small daughter Jessie; her
sisters, Mrs. Clarence (Lucy) Snead and thirteen year old
Bertha Hurt; my Dad's first cousins, Daisy and Carrie
Copeland; and his best friend and distant kinsman, Fred
Kincaid.

**Photograph 3 Mom and Pop near their Wedding Day. These
pictures always hung in our family home.**

When they were married Pop was twenty-three years of age and Mom was nineteen. They started housekeeping in a small Kanawha County community of Morocco where Pop worked in a coal mine. The town is no longer in existence, or at least I can't find it on present day maps.

They didn't start their married life as paupers. In a letter to Mom, her sister, my Aunt Lucy Snead, remarks about the nice wedding gift of $100.00 Pop's father had given them. This was a sizable amount of money for that time. Pop's timekeeping books show that about five years later, in 1908, a daily wage was $1.75 to $2.00, and a week's wages based on 60 hours made up of six ten-hour shifts, was about $12.00. Monthly rent for a company house was $4.00. The monthly fuel bill for coal was $1.50, and the monthly fee for doctor's services was $1.00. One page of entries has Pop with an unbelievable monthly total of 291 hours of labor, 141 of them in a period of thirteen consecutive days. That one month he had earned $72.75. At that time there were three children, and the monthly store account for the family was about $35.00. This information makes the $100.00 received as a wedding gift look pretty good.

My Mom and Dad were from two rather ordinary families, the Copelands, and the Hurts. Both surnames were English or Irish, but there were other influences, as would be expected, since both families arrived in the United States before the American Revolutionary War. We can trace the Hurts to the early part of the eighteenth century, and the Copelands to the middle of that century. Mom's mother was born Bettie Ruth Field, and the Hurts, Fields, and a third family, the Tuckers, were intertwined for several generations, where first cousins married on more than one occasion. The Hurts point proudly to their English heritage and to their status as eligible "Daughters of the American Revolution", but rarely to the dubious record of intermar-

14

riage. We sometimes joked that their lineage was so great that they were too good for the commoners around them, so were left with only kinfolk to marry.

Photograph 4 My maternal grandparents Garland and Betty Field Hurt.

On the Hurt side, Mom's parents (my grandparents) were first cousins. The intermarriage was so pervasive and longstanding, that of my four sets of great-great grandparents on the Hurt side, every couple consists of at least one Hurt. There were no obvious consequences of this intermarriage, although when anyone in the family acted peculiar in any way, this was always cited as the reason.

The Hurts were tall people. Mom was tall, 5 feet 10½ inches, and weighed around 200 pounds. I think she weighed around 145 pounds when she was married. Her hair was dark brown, and she had pretty brown eyes. She turned gray at a very early age, and I can't remember her except when her hair was gray. She had regular features, and a beautiful expression.

Bertha, Vernice, and Faye inherited the Hurt height, and were all around five feet ten inches tall. My three brothers who survived to be adults were well over six feet tall, only I got the more modest Copeland dimension of around five feet seven inches. When Mom died in 1976, the Reverend Shirley Donnally, a frequent contributor to the Beckley Post Herald and the Raleigh Register, devoted the following column to her:

LADY HELPED MAKE THE WORLD RICHER

Another old friend of long years left the shores of time and put out to sea. This time it was Mrs. Luther Copeland, nee Nannie Hurt (August 9, 1884- Feb 23, 1976) who answered the summons from on high. Mrs. Copeland was a native of the Meadow Fork Creek Valley in the Sanger section near Oak Hill. Her parents were Garland and Bettie Hurt, both of blessed memory.

16

*Few people live as long and as well as did
Mrs. Copeland, whose life was 91 years, eight
months and two weeks long.*

*Mrs. Copeland had a brother named John
Calvin Hurt who was the greatest handshaker I ever
knew. He was doorkeeper in the U.S. Senate the
time two Puerto Rican terrorists got by and shot up
the Senate.*

*"Cal" Hurt, as he was known, held many
public offices in Fayette County. Once he was de-
tailed as deputy sheriff to transport an old friend of
mine to the penitentiary.*

*To get to Moundsville they took the C&O to
Huntington where they had to wait until 9 a.m. the
next day to get the B&O to Moundsville. Cal Hurt
knew the prisoner and knew the old fellow had a
fine son who lived in Huntington.*

*Hurt told this man that he was supposed to
confine him in jail until the train ran the next
morning. But, a trusting soul, Cal told the prisoner
if he would promise to meet him at the B&O depot
in the morning he could spend the night with his
son.*

*Cal Hurt told me that when he got to the de-
pot at 8:55 A.M., that morning, he saw the prisoner
walking the platform in a restless manner, feeling
his officer would miss the train that was going to
take him to the penitentiary.*

Mrs. Copeland's parents were natives of Bedford County, VA. They were Garland and Betty Hurt. Prior to her marriage to Garland Hurt, Betty was the girl friend of John Quincy Dickenson in Bedford.

Dickenson tried to induce her to become his wife but his pleas fell on deaf ears. Instead, Betty married Garland Hurt. It was the parting of the ways for the young couple. John Dickenson migrated to Charleston where he became president of the Kanawha Valley Bank until he died.

At the time of his passing, J.Q. Dickenson, an old Confederate soldier, was a very wealthy man. Garland Hurt, and his wife Betty, moved to the Meadow Fork section where their long lives were spent in only moderate circumstances.

It was just another case of where "It might have been" different had another marriage taken place instead of the one that did.

Mrs. Copeland was indeed an elect lady— one of the best I have ever known. She gave to the world a noble family. The world is better because Nannie Copeland lived her nearly 92 years.

God rest her soul in endless peace.

The Copelands were of Irish descent, as was my paternal grandmother, Emma Ellen Hill Copeland. Her ancestry includes some Indian blood through the Estep family in Kentucky. She had died in 1880, about three weeks after Pop was born, and Grandpa Copeland never remarried, but raised the two children, Pop and Lettie, who was four years older than Pop.

Photograph 5 My paternal grandparents Emma Ellen Hill and Winfield Copeland.

Pop was of medium build, about 5 feet 10 inches tall, weighing around 160 pounds. He had dark brown hair, gray eyes, and a rather large nose. I thought he was hand-some. He was a good host, but did not like to visit people or attend social gatherings. He was very stable emotionally but was quick tempered.

Pop's father, my Grandpa Copeland, spent most of his years living with Aunt Lettie and Uncle Henry Gross. He was a devout Christian who would not put up with any drinking, or what he considered to be non-Christian be-havior. This of course, included profanity, which some-times got Pop in trouble with him since Pop was known to so express himself in his younger pre-conversion days. I always thought Uncle Henry got a raw deal since Grandpa was clearly the master of the household, but I never saw any sign of resentment from Uncle Henry.

Grandpa was a very strict man, and particularly strict with my dad, insisting that he go to church every Sunday. I don't think Grandpa had much understanding for children, or young people. I think he may have been too strict, but he certainly instilled in my father good traits of character. At his death, he had been a widower for sixty-three years. In her book, Vernice reprints the eulogy, written by her in 1943 to Grandpa Copeland, which ran in the Nicholas County Chronicle where she worked:

Winfield Copeland

At the age of nineteen Mr. Copeland consecrated his life to the Lord and joined the Gauley Bridge Baptist Church (where his funeral service was conducted some seventy years later). No eulogy need be composed for him: he wrote it himself in the virtuous life he lived day by day.

Quite early in life he learned that conquering self is

Photograph 6 Grandpa Winfield Copeland in 1930 at the age of 77.

man's biggest victory, and he won that victory. His was an exemplary life, one of clean, almost stern habits but one of humble service to his fellow man. Left with two motherless children, he tried to be both father and mother to them, and to instill in them his own love and reverence for God. His off-spring may well say: "The lines are fallen to me in pleasant places; yea, I have a goodly heritage." As in his home, so at his place of work he testified regularly of the love of Christ. Not given to foolish jesting or idle talk, and quick to rebuke any who spoke irreverently of his Savior, yet so powerfully did his own life exemplify his doctrine of conduct that he won the respect of even the most ungodly to such an extent that they refrained from profanity in his hearing. On one occasion, as a fellow log worker lay dying of injuries sustained when a log crushed him, he called for Mr. Copeland to pray with him to show him the way.

Short moments before his own death, when he knew that his time was fast slipping away, Mr. Copeland spoke to a weeping loved one, "O please don't cry. You must rejoice. Laugh with me." And joyously he laughed aloud, glorying in anticipation of the won-der of the reunion with the wife of his youth, but far more greatly rejoicing that he would soon behold his Savior whom he knew and loved beyond meas-ure, and in whose steps he had faithfully followed.

This bit of verse Mr. Copeland carried for years in his billfold, often reading it to friends:

O Death, thou had conquered me;
I by thy hand am slain;
But Jesus Christ has conquered thee,
And I shall rise again!

The Copelands, when we can first document them, were in Tennessee, of Irish origin, probably by way of North Carolina. Carolyn Caplinger, in her Internet genealogy of the Copeland Family, makes the following statement: "David Copeland is believed to have been born in Ireland. After coming to America, he became a soldier in the Revolutionary War from North Carolina. Following the war, he settled in Maury County, TN, on bounty land received for helping in the establishment of American Independence. His wife was Jane Craig, probably sister of Captain David Craig of the Revolutionary War, who also received bounty land in Maury County. From records of legal and business transactions, we learned the two families were close. This was especially true of James Craig and Anthony M. Copeland. Although David Copeland died in Arkansas, his property was in Tennessee, and his will was probated in Maury County, Tennessee."

Pop's great grandfather, Hezekiah Balch Copeland, was supposedly dispatched from Tennessee to Washington, DC, by his father David, to take a load of hogs to market. Disaster struck in what is now Fayette County, West Virginia, and the cargo was lost. Hezekiah never returned home. I don't know when this occurred, but Hezekiah was born in 1789, so I would guess this occurred somewhere around 1810. This was reflected in the aforementioned will of his father, David, where Hezekiah was left the paltry sum of five dollars while the other siblings received substantial money and property. Pop's grandfather, An-thony, was a farmer who lived his entire life in Fayette County, West Virginia, and was apparently a landowner. There was one other mention of property in the family lore. Pop's father, Winfield, apparently staked claim to some land in one of the more remote areas of Nicholas County, and asked a neighbor who was traveling to the county seat in Summersville to register his claim. Years later it turned

22

out that the neighbor had registered the claim in his own name, and Grandpa lost the land.

Pop's mother's family, the Hills, were an impressive group with ancestors prominent in early American history. Several fought in the Revolutionary war, and some were officers of note. One branch of that family is the Rutherfords, whose lineage traces back for ten centuries into British and French nobility. In the eighteenth century, our line to the Rutherfords crosses the daughter of respected landowner, Bartholemew Vawter. We have a copy of his will, which was executed September 17, 1717, in Essex County, Virginia. Vawter appears to have been seventy-seven years of age at the time of his death. The famous Vauter church in Essex County, founded two years after his death, is doubtlessly named for the family. We were told by the Essex County Clerk, that the spelling of the family name was

Photograph 7 Vauter's Church in Essex County, Virginia.

changed because ex-slaves were using the original name. Vawter's daughter Margaret would have been my fifth great-grandmother, while Bartholomew Vawter would be my sixth great-grandfather. Vawter was born in Edward County, England, in 1640, while Margaret was probably also born in England about 1672.

Chapter Four
My First School

We moved back to Sanger in Fayette County shortly after
Faye was born, and Pop went back to the mines after a few
years away from them. Not long after we moved back to
Fayette County, Mom broke her leg one day while carrying
Faye in her arms. Vern and I cried and cried, because
somewhere we came up with the idea that the leg would
have to be amputated. Pop hired a woman to help Mom,
but after a short stint, Mom dismissed the help, mostly to
alleviate the added strain her wages placed on the household budget. Mom hobbled on crutches to carry on household duties. I had started to school that year, and with
Bertha and me both in school that left just Vernice home
with Mom, on crutches, and Faye, a small baby. Vern felt
very mistreated because she felt all the burden of looking
after the house, and with Faye on her hip. That was a very
big job for a child of about four years of age.

I was really excited about starting school, particularly since
I would be with Bert, to whom I was strongly attached.
The school at Sanger, like most of the country schools of
that day, was a one-room or two-room structure with the
six to eight elementary grades being taught by a single
teacher simultaneously. This particular school had two
rooms, with grades 1-4 in one room, and grades 5-8 in the
other. The structure usually included space, crudely parti-
tioned off, where a table held a water bucket with a dipper
for drinking (everyone drank from the same dipper), and a
wash basin for washing hands. There were also nails on the
wall for hanging coats or other outer garments, and space
for galoshes or boots.

The main room had rows of desks permanently attached to
the floor. The desk consisted of two detached parts, first,

the writing desk with a compartment underneath for books and papers, and holes for ink bottles, and then the folding seat which was attached to the next desk behind. Two students often shared the seat and desk, side by side. In this room there was a pot-bellied coal or wood burning stove to heat the room. The usual blackboard covered the front wall of the room with windows along at least one of the two sides. Ages or classes were segregated into small groups around the room, and class recitations always spilled over, so the younger children absorbed at least some of what was being taught to the older children. Of course, there were boy's and girl's outhouses, usually on opposite sides of the building, and there was of necessity a coal or wood shed for fuel as appropriate.

I still remember my first teacher, a Miss Daisy Horan. Her sister Alice was the principal, teaching the upper grades. Ms. Horan was strict, and I was deathly afraid of her. Sadly, she died of tuberculosis a few years later, and my siblings always attributed her untimely death to the strain I had put on her.

Photograph 8 Group picture from Sanger School my first year; I am in the first row, seventh from the left, partially behind Bert.

I'll never forget as long as I live, the day I was supposed to tell a story to my classmates in the first grade. I chose Cinderella as my story to tell. I said she went to the ball game, not knowing the meaning of the word "ball". The teacher gently corrected me, and the children didn't laugh, nor do anything to ridicule me, but because I was so overly sensitive, I was terribly embarrassed.

Many of my teachers opened school with scripture reading, everyone repeating the Lord's Prayer in unison and sometimes singing a hymn. Subjects taught were reading, writing, arithmetic, civics, spelling, English, geography and history. School began at 9 a.m., and dismissed at 4 p.m., with an hour for lunch and two recess periods of 15 minutes—one in the forenoon and one in the afternoon.

Pupils had to pass an eighth grade diploma test in order to graduate from eighth grade (there was no graduation ceremony) and enter high school. I think the diploma was mailed from the county seat, but the test for the diploma was alike for everyone in the state.

My teachers were, without exception, very dedicated people with high morals—good role models who reinforced good character traits taught by our parents. They demanded good behavior, and if anyone dared disobey, he might be whipped with a large switch cut from the branch of a tree. Less severe infractions called for less severe punishment such as standing in the corner, or sitting on a bench with the word "Lazy" printed on it.

I don't remember being punished at school. I guess I was too timid to stand the embarrassment, and too cowardly to stand the pain.

I was always so timid and shy and hung onto Bert everywhere she went. This got me in trouble one day as Bert, Dallas Hurt, our first cousin, and I were walking home from school. I was nearly run over by a motor (the coal mines equivalent of a small locomotive) pulling a long string of coal cars. We, along with a group of other children, were coming home from school. I was only six and Bert and Dallas were eight. We walked along a track on which a motor pulled cars filled with coal from a nearby mine. On the way, there was a trestle, which spanned a very small creek. As we came to the trestle we heard the motor coming. Some of the children crossed the trestle, and others waited for this motor to pass by. Bert and Dallas crossed and I followed, and fell in the last step of the trestle. By this time the motor was very close, but the motorman couldn't stop, because it was down grade and the heavily loaded coal cars kept pushing it on. The men on the motor started yelling, and the children started screaming. Just in time Dallas grabbed me, and pulled me off the track. Some of the children said they turned their heads because they didn't want to see me get killed. The brakeman told my dad that he was just ready to jump off and try to save me when Dallas pulled me off the track.

Bert and Dallas were fast friends, but in my eyes, something of a behavior problem at the little school in Sanger. I viewed them as lazy and knew they whispered. I was embarrassed when they would have to sit on the "lazy bench" for misbehavior.

Our stay at Sanger lasted just about one year, and then we returned to Swiss. One of my most memorable recollections of Swiss was of the big steam engines that would run from Charleston to Swiss. These would pull passenger cars as well as coal cars, and always bringing up the rear, was the red caboose. Vern and I would be on the porch of the company store, most everyday, watching for the train to come in. As it pulled in, we moved closer to the tracks, and the engineer would watch for us, and would release a cloud of steam, completely covering us, much to our delight.

Photograph 9 The children as we were at Swiss. L-R Faye, Vern, Bert, and me.

In 1913 we saw our first automobile. Dr. Timberlake from Jodie owned it. He came across the Gauley River on a ferry with his car to visit a patient at Swiss. We lined up to watch him. He stopped, or nearly stopped, when he got to where we were standing, and promised us a ride on his return trip. We were greatly disappointed when he drove by us on his return trip with his eyes fixed straight ahead, leaving us standing, watching as he disappeared from sight.

Mom used to take us to visit Grandpa and Grandma Hurt. We would travel from Swiss to where they lived in Sanger. We would ride the train to Thurmond where someone met us with a horse drawn vehicle. Pop couldn't go, as he worked six days a week, and couldn't get off from work. The train ride was very special to me as was Grandma's good cooking—her jams and jellies, ham, biscuits, and loaves of homemade bread.

Another memory, not so pleasant, was our fear of drunks. I think Mom had planted a real fear of people who were drinking in us at an early age, and there was probably plenty of drinking and rowdiness going on in Swiss, which was a large logging camp. I suspect I instilled this same fear in my own children, because they had a rather intense fear of some folks who lived at the head of Drews Creek, who often drove by when we suspected they had been drinking. I also remember the fear that I would have watching Pop scale the logs in the pond at the big saw mill in Swiss. I always had a fear of someone knocking on the door, telling us Pop had been drowned or killed.

I'll never forget when our family would play a guessing game in which the leader gave someone's initials and the others guessed who it was. Of course, the one guessing correctly, became the new leader. This became quite difficult sometimes. For instance: there was an old man who lived in the community whose last name was Beaver. None of us knew his first or middle name. The leader (I don't know who it was, maybe Mom, who was quite good at this game) said. Who's OMB? (Old Man Beaver) Someone finally guessed. We all got so we were pretty clever at this game. We also played card games, we sang together, hymns and ballads, and sometimes we just talked, and we loved for our parents to tell us stories about themselves when they were growing up.

We didn't have popcorn because you couldn't buy it in the stores, but we often had parched corn, which was fixed like popcorn. It was regular field corn, heated in butter in a skillet or kettle, with a lid. It had to be moved backward and forward on the hot stove until it partially popped. It was like popcorn kernel that didn't completely pop.

When I was very young, Bert was the typical older sister to me. I clung to her and thought she knew everything. After the measles left her with a crippled foot that made it difficult for her to run, she began to be more interested in indoor things to do, while I began to like outdoor games. Vern, although she was two years younger than I was, soon grew until she was as large as I, and people thought we were twins. Mom often dressed us alike, and we certainly were a lot alike in our likes and dislikes. We were both "tomboys", and were the ones who went to the store and post office, etc. Bert loved each new baby, and chose to look after the baby. We thought she did it to get out of washing dishes, but after she grew up, she said it was because she loved each new baby. She matured so much earlier than I, that she was not interested in Vernice's or my "childish" ways, nor were we interested in her "grown up" ways, consequently Vern and I "cliqued" together, and excluded both Bert and Faye. Faye was always very mature for her age. At age 4, she checked to see if we older girls had done our chores. She was always very conscientious, and had a delightful sense of humor.

When I was nearly eight years old, on March 4, 1914, another baby arrived in our home at Swiss. Vern and I had seen the doctor arrive carrying a little black bag, and we knew right then where they had gotten Lowell when they came and told us we had a baby brother. Lowell was such a red-skinned baby, that when we first saw him, Vern said "Wonder where the doctor found a little Indian baby?" Lowell Ellis was quite a novelty since he had four older sisters. Lowell Ellis was named for Pop and the doctor who delivered him.

Faye had been born after Garland's death, and was, understandably, very spoiled as a result. Lowell had the same dark brown eyes that Faye had, and despite Pop's remark that "If any dark-eyed babies were born here, they were going packing", the two "black-eyed babies" were, to the contrary, spoiled rotten.

We moved to Drennen a while after Lowell was born. Lowell's four older sisters really doted on him. I remember how we would dress him up and put a toy pipe in his mouth, and a railroad cap on his head and take him to the door to watch for the train to go by. Pop and Uncle Henry, the engineer, were on the train, and both would wave and Uncle Henry would blow the whistle and send forth a blast of steam, much to the delight of all involved.

At Drennen we lived in a "shanty car" for a time. Shanty cars were boxcar-sized portable shacks. The company placed them on flat cars, actually log cars, and moved them from site to site as they were needed. In her book, my sister, Vernice, remembers that we actually had three cars arranged in a "U-shape" with interconnecting doors between them. As if the shanty car arrangement wasn't crowded enough, another baby boy was added to the family. After two "black-eyed babies", a towhead, Edwin Luther, arrived January 24th, 1916, when I was ten years old, and things got very crowded.

After Pop's wages afforded a house, we moved into the "Jim Drennen Place". It was a family house, and we were a large family by this time. Jim Drennen must have built a new house for his family, because I can remember a baby being born to his wife, and the need for someone to help her with the baby until she got stronger from giving birth. Mom couldn't do without Bert's help at home, so she sent

Vern and me. I can remember getting up and making biscuits for the Drennen Family, and can remember the wonderful cured hams. I was ten years old and Vernice was eight.

Vern and I were beginning to think there was something wrong with Bert about this time. She would primp all the time, even before going to bed. When we asked her what she was doing that for, her reply was "You don't know, the house might catch on fire tonight, and I would want my hair to look nice." We would taunt her saying "The plain old way is the best old way." She would reply "The 'fixey' old way is the best old way."

Photograph 10 Group photo from Drennen School. I am the girl centered under the state flag, Vern is the second girl left of me, Bert is the third girl to her left, and Faye might be the girl with bangs on the far right.

One of life's most embarrassing moments (for a child) happened to me at Drennen. Pop was going to the store, and was going to buy pencils for the next week. I told him I wouldn't need one, because I would earn one the next day by getting the head mark in spelling. The head mark was obtained by outspelling everyone else in a spelling bee. I was a very good speller, and up to that point had missed just three words in my first three years in school, a word a year, but that winning streak came to a disappointing end that day. I was beaten, and didn't get a pencil. I couldn't stand to face Pop and tell him I had missed a word in spelling, and besides that, I didn't have a pencil. The others would tease me by recalling the three previous misspelled words in a little chant "I went out in a <u>field</u> on <u>Wednesday</u> and sat on a <u>cushion</u>." That incident ended my keeping track of misspelled words.

My father was an honest, hard-working man, a devoted father, a man of high principles, and very protective of his family. We children knew he loved Mom and us, although he didn't tell us he loved us but demonstrated it in so many ways. Some things that stand out in my memory about my relationship with my dad are: (1) Learning to clean fish and squirrels, and to pluck and clean wild turkey and grouse so I could be near him and talk to him as we worked together. (2) Feeling so protected when he was near. (3) Having a terrible fear that he might get injured or killed when he worked at hazardous jobs. (4) Listening to stories about his childhood and feeling so proud of him when my friends liked the stories too. (5) Always wanting to do well in school so he would be proud of me.

One special thing I remember was when Pop would come home from his day's shift at work. Vern and I would run to meet him. He always saved something he knew we would like from his lunch that day. The special treats would be in his lunch pail, maybe cake, fried chicken, or perhaps fried apple pie. We would take the treats from the lunch pail and as we ate we would walk with him carrying his lunch pail. I am sure he would have liked these goodies himself, but he didn't want to disappoint us. There is also the possibility that Mom had packed a little something extra just with this in mind.

Pop was very special to me growing up, and although I loved Mom, I just felt Pop was special. I remember at Drennen one morning, he got up to go to work and sat in a chair and said, uncharacteristically "Nan could you hurry with breakfast, I am starving!" After he sat down in the chair, he couldn't get up. Mom helped him to the bed, but he was delirious. Mom sent us to get the doctor, and the doctor told us he had pneumonia. Pop was very sick, and our house was unusually quite for several days as we were all so scared, afraid he would die. Finally, Mom told us he was better, and I can still remember feeling like I would just burst with happiness.

I believe Pop could have made a good surgeon. When I was in high school I did quite a bit of sewing. On one occasion I sewed through my finger, breaking off a sewing machine needle in my finger. The eye part of the needle was just barely peeping through the underside of my finger, and the bigger part was even with my finger nail on the top, making it very difficult to get hold of to remove it. Pop gave me a choice of having him cut it out, or going to a doctor to have him cut it out. I chose Pop, and he went to work. He sterilized a straight razor, and tied a tourniquet on my wrist. He worked quickly and very proficiently. He cut the bottom of my finger until he exposed enough of the needle, then pulled it out with pliers or some other tool. I had no trouble with it at all. It seemed to me that Pop could always solve our problems, whatever the need was, but especially when we had wounds of any kind. We all knew we had my dad's protection, and felt secure in the knowl-

35

edge that no one would try anything that might bring on his wrath.

Growing up, I had problems with homework, I felt that my clothes were not "good enough", I had acne, and other problems common to teen agers. Mom was always a good listener. She was very good to help with my homework. I think she explained math more thoroughly than my teachers did, so that I understood fractions, long division, addition with carrying, etc. I think the fourth grade was the hardest grade, especially for me in math. We also started studying history then, but Mom continued to be a big help with homework, even when I was in high school. Luckily Mom was a good seamstress, so she was able to solve the problems of not having suitable clothes. She sat up all night, many times, in order to get dresses ready for us girls.

Mom also had a sense of humor, which is often overlooked in the tragedies of her life. To illustrate this, I offer the following story she told. A neighbor lady, unnamed for obvious reasons, was having some female problems. Her symptoms included severe itching, foul odor, and probable infection. After some delay, she went to the doctor for help. After an examination, he began to hint to her that her problem was a simple matter of hygiene. He said to her "Madame, tell me about how often you bathe." To this she responded, "Well I bathe often enough, I wash down as far as possible, and I wash up as far as possible." At that the doctor declared, "Well then I think we have found the trouble, you'll just have to start washing 'possible' too!"

Mom had a deep faith, and I think it showed in the serenity of her expression. She hated profanity and vulgar language. We were not allowed to use such words as "gosh" or "darn" as they bordered on profanity, and were not "ladylike". I think this is the very reason I remembered the above humorous story, because it was so out of character for her. Mom was a very intelligent woman, with a real talent for expressing herself in writing. She had taught school one year before she married. Mom did not attend many social events because she didn't have suitable clothes a lot of the time, and she was so busy trying to take care of her large family. I think Mom's best character trait was her deep faith in God.

When Bert, Vern and I got home from school, "Bossy" Faye would meet us. She would hardly let us in the door when she would start: "Children, have you got the kindling in? When are you going to get the coal and water? Don't you know Mom needs help?" We would seethe in anger to have our four-year-old sister bossing us around.

I'll never forget our grocery store. It was the typical country general store. We must have lived about a mile from the store, and my sister Vernice and I did most of the shopping. We just gave the clerk the list Mom had written, and the owner filled the list. The inventory seemed to include everything the customer needed, such as hardware, shoes, dress print, etc. There was no refrigeration, so it didn't carry meats or dairy products. Customers had their own meats and dairy products. I know we had chickens, but no other animals to supply meat. Mom occasionally bought salt fish. It came in a wooden keg about a gallon in size. The fish were packed in salt, and required soaking for about 24 hours, with frequent changes of water, in order to be edible. She also bought canned salmon. If Pop could get a little time off from work, he would go hunting. He was usually successful in killing some kind of game such as quail, rabbit, or squirrel to help supply meat. Pinto beans helped supply our protein. Mom bought canned milk from the store, and we bought butter and buttermilk from a neighbor lady. We bought flour and meal from the store.

37

Bread was homemade. Mom sometimes made rolls and loaves of bread using yeast, but mostly we had biscuits and cornbread.

I think what most impressed me at the grocery store was the candy display in glass jars something like our cookie jars. It was sold piece by piece. I think it was a penny apiece although it might have been cheaper. We didn't get to buy much candy, because it was very difficult for Pop to pay our monthly bills when he got his payday; however, as you will see, not buying candy often, didn't necessarily mean we went without.

Bossy Faye decided she could go anywhere and do anything Vern and I did, and she got lots of encouragement from Mom. We had little desire to take her with us, one reason being she tired easily, and we had to carry her, because she would go on a "sitdown strike" if we didn't. Mom would make us take her to the store and post office, after she would beg and promise we wouldn't have to carry her anymore. Each time it was the same, she would pull her sit-down strike, and we, mainly Vern, would have to carry her. We told Mom, truthfully, that she embarrassed us, because she would cry for candy at the store. We had finally found a way to a little payback for all the putting up with her. Mom gave us a good "out." She told us we couldn't get her any candy unless she cried for it. So we made sure she cried. We would say, "Faye, honey, would you like some candy?" Of course, her answer was "yes". Then we would come back with, "Well you can't have any." Now what 4-year old wouldn't cry? Faye didn't disappoint us, and we had to get enough for the rest of us too. Soon Mom realized what was happening and as everyone knows – "all good things come to an end." I never felt Mom or Pop really cared a great deal, because one way or another, we seemed to get sweets fairly often.

One regular candy binge was when Pop settled his accounts at two grocery stores, where by tradition; each would give a huge bag of candy.

When I was a youngster, Christmas was quieter, and not so commercialized as it is today. We did not have a tree, nor did we hang our stockings. In our younger years, we girls usually got dolls or games. Our family was very poor, but in spite of this, we children always had at least one gift. We had candy, nuts, and some fruits—apples and oranges. My parents did not give gifts to each other, instead they used the money to buy gifts for us children. We always had a good Christmas dinner with plenty of pies and cakes. I don't remember having turkey. Often we had roast chicken and mashed potatoes, other vegetables, and Mom's good homemade biscuits.

On Christmas Eve, we dutifully went to bed early so Santa could bring our gifts, although we knew (thanks to Bert), that Pop and Mom were the real Santa. Pretending sleep, we waited until Pop and Mom came in with a light and checked to see if we were asleep. Convinced that we were asleep, they put the gifts out, and went to bed. After what seemed like a long time, we'd slip out of bed to see what "Santa" left. Daring only a swift look, we'd creep back to bed, spending a long, almost sleepless, night, until we could get up in the early morning to act surprised at our "first look" at our gifts.

One of the best Christmas gifts I ever got was when I was about six years old. It was a beautiful china doll with long brown curls. She was in an elegant lacy blue dress, and I thought she was beautiful. Unhappily, I didn't get to keep her very long. Vernice dropped her and broke her on Christmas day. Mom told her she had to give me her doll, but she cried so much, I didn't take her doll. Besides, no doll was as pretty as mine, and none could take her place. Churches and schools did put on very nice Christmas programs in which we participated. They also usually gave out a small bag of treats to each child.

From Drennen, our next move was to Zela. We were getting closer to Summersville with each move. Summersville was the county seat of Nicholas County, and the high school was located there. That year in Zela, I attended the Bell school. The teacher and students at Bell school treated us as outsiders. We were foreigners from the works, since this was a farming community, and all the children had lived there for their entire lives, and they all knew each other. I believe the teacher knew all the students well, and felt they were performing well academically. When we went in, and out-performed them, we made enemies of all except the teacher's teenaged brother, who had a crush on Bert. The teacher and her brother would conspire to see that he sat very close to her on the recitation bench. He got many jabs with pencils, but endured them in silence for the pleasure of sitting next to Bert. All of the jabs and rejection were observed by his sister who made life unpleasant, not only for Bert, but for Vern and me also. We were happy to learn we would be moving before the beginning of a new school term.

Although school wasn't very pleasant, the summer proved to be filled with new experiences and adventures. Pop taught us to fish in Peters' creek, and frequently, Vern and I caught many nice-sized bass and suckers, which made for very good eating for the family. Bert never cared for fishing, but really took to swimming. Bert helped Mom with the smaller children, while Vern and I did the outside chores.

Photograph 11 Photo from Zela School. I am the girl in the center with a hand on my shoulder, Bert is next, to the right and back one row, Vern is the fifth girl from the left, possibly kneeling. Vern and I have identical dresses.

The Baptist Church at Zela represents a milestone in my life, because it was where I became a Christian, when I was about 12 years old.

Our days were filled that summer with trips to the store and post office, going to neighbors for dairy products, picking berries, bringing in water, coal, and kindling wood, besides our catching fish to feed the family. Often our trips had added pleasures, such as swinging on neighbor's gates, the kind that crossed roads leading up long lanes to houses, so far away it was hard for us to be detected. At one such home, we felt secure, and really got thrills on the swinging gate before we went to the home to get buttermilk. On arriving, we found we were not far enough away and had been seen. The farmer's wife let us know she had caught us, and she also informed us, "Farmers don't like children

41

swinging on their gates, and sometimes they whip them."
After this, I wasn't about to go for buttermilk by myself.

One day when Mom sent us for buttermilk, she instructed
us to go straight there, and not play around. On the way we
saw some wild grapevines that looked just right for swinging, and they had even been cut for that purpose. Vern was
afraid to try, so I told her I would go first, and if they held
me, surely they would hold her. I swung out for a thrilling
ride. Vern grabbed the vine, took a big run, and went
through the air.... and kept going. The vine slipped from
the branches, and she tumbled to the ground, landing on a
tree stump that had a sharp cut edge. She got a bad cut and
was bleeding. She turned to go home, but I told her if she
did I would rock her, which meant I would throw rocks at
her. She knew I meant it, because I was not about to go get
milk at that house by myself. We had to make up a tale to
tell Mom when Vern returned home cut and bleeding. As I
recall, we told her Vern tripped and fell on a sapling stump
by the side of the road. Our story was partially true, and
Mom never questioned it, but we felt guilty nevertheless.

It is obvious that despite the many chores Vern and I had to
do, we found plenty of opportunities for exploration and
adventure. One "forgettable" adventure happened while we
were picking berries with a neighbor, Aunt Jenny Nickols,
who always accompanied us to the berry field. She was not
a blood aunt, but was called "Aunt" by the whole community. We were picking berries some distance from Aunt
Jenny in this very large berry field, when we spied a flock
of half-grown turkeys soaring to the hill opposite where we
were picking. We were very excited over the first wild
turkeys we had ever seen. We began to slip up behind
them, and getting close enough, we gave chase, and caught
two of them. Vern held them, while I took a sharp stone
and severed their heads. We quickly hid them in a hollow

tree, where we could find them when we finished picking berries. The season for turkey hunting was over so we wanted to be secretive about our catch. We knew Mom and Pop would be proud of our ability to catch wild turkey and we knew we would enjoy eating them. After hiding our catch, we returned to picking berries. We were scared and horrified, when Aunt Jenny mentioned seeing Frank Graves' nice flock of young turkeys that he was raising to take to market. She had seen them flying over the hill from his farm. How were we supposed to know tame turkeys could fly? Well two of them would never fly again, and as far as I know, they are still resting in that hollow log. The story of our turkey hunt was never mentioned until we were grown and away from home. Even then, I don't believe we ever told Mom and Pop.

The 1918-19 influenza pandemic hit the Copeland family hard in 1918, as this, the nation's worst natural disaster gripped the rest of the nation, and indeed most of the world. All members of the household were real sick, but I believe Vern and I were probably the worst. Mom and Pop were both sick, but while all the rest of us could go to bed, they didn't have that choice, since they had to constantly doctor the rest of us. Pop had done a lot of the doctoring up till that time, but it seems Mom did the doctoring then, at least for Vern and me. We were put in a bed together, and it seems like she worked with us day and night for a long while. Our bed stay lasted at least two weeks. I felt like Mom did most of the care because we were beginning to develop physically, and it would have been awkward for Pop to apply the Vick's salve to our chests, and look after us like we needed at that time. I can't remember ever having had a headache like that, before or since. I must have had a very high fever, because my hair came out. I can remember all I could eat, or even think of eating, was canned tomatoes. I can't remember medicines they used,

43

but we did have a doctor visit us and leave medicine, which Mom administered. Most of the doctoring in that day and time was done with home remedies.

At the end of that summer, we moved to another location in Zela and a new school. I was eleven years old and that year, unlike the past year, I made some new friends. Among them were Louise Carden, the doctor's daughter, Nellie Gray, and Pauline Neil. Louise always had so many books, and she shared them, and I really enjoyed reading. In her house was a parlor, never used, kept just for company. On one occasion, I remember going to her house, wading the creek to get there, and as I stepped in the door of the parlor, now bare footed, I felt something crawl over my bare foot. I looked down and saw a house snake, and nearly fainted.

Photograph 12 Zela School. On the back of the picture, very childish handwriting identifies most of the people: "first row Pauline Neil; Louise Carden; Daisy Copeland; Nelly Gray; Vernice Copeland; Maisie Martin. 2nd row ? Legg; Ruby Painter; ? Legg; Maggie Leacher; Bertha Copeland ; ? Legg; and Cora Painter. Boy in the window is H(?) Martin." Writer who is likely a sibling of Maggie Leacher couldn't tell the three Legg girls apart.

On another occasion, we had several days of heavy rains, and the creek kept us completely cut off from Louise's house. When the creek was down, Mom sent me to find out about Louise's little brother who had been ill. I went to the door, and asked Louise's mother how he was, and imagine how I felt when she told me he had died, and they had buried him.

I remember Nellie being good in math, and since I was good in math also, we shared a desk, and had a good time working our problems. Nellie brought me an apple every day. They were such good apples that I can still remember the good taste. They called them Milam apples, but I can't think of any apple today that compares to them. Pauline Neil was really a rival of mine. We would work very hard to keep abreast of each other. Even though she was a grade ahead of me in school, we competed with each other in that one-room school. Louise was also a year ahead of me, but Nellie and I were in the same grade.

The teacher there was a very colorful character; by colorful, I mean his dress. He wore an army uniform, as he had just gotten out of the service in World War I. Of course it was then called the World War. Along with the uniform, he always wore red socks. He started coming to our house real often. Bert told Mom he was too interested in her, but Mom didn't believe her since she was just about 13 years old, but Bert kept insisting. The school year passed without any indication Mom could see. Then about three years later, Vern and I went to the post office to get the mail. In the mail was a letter to Bert from her old teacher. We proceeded to open the letter and read it. He was proposing to Bert, and we couldn't wait to get home to announce it. Mom realized then that Bert must have been right, he was too interested in her. He hadn't seen her since, so the fire still lingered from three years earlier. Mom helped her to write a letter of refusal to his proposal, explaining she was too young to think about marriage. Bert would have been about 16 years old when she received the letter.

We attended Zela School for two terms and part of a third. Faye started school our second term there when she was five years old. We moved to Enon when I was in seventh grade. I had part of a year at Enon School before I went to high school at Nicholas County High School in Summersville.

At Enon, we got drinking water from a spring about two hundred yards from the house. One night Pop was going to get two buckets of water, so I went along to carry a flashlight. As he was getting the water, he felt something hit his thumb, and shining the light to see what it was, he found a copperhead snake. It really hadn't broken the skin, and he wasn't worried at all. He proceeded to kill the snake and go on about fetching the water. Although he didn't worry, I did. I cried and cried, and begged him to go to a doctor. I was sure he would die. He didn't go, and had no ill effects. The water in that spring was so cool and so good to drink, but I always remembered the copperhead incident, and trips after dark to get water ceased.

We children were taught right from wrong, and as we matured we were pretty much on an honor system. We knew they trusted us, and we didn't want to do anything to betray that trust. I don't think they were too strict, but we girls felt that they became more lax with the younger children—the three boys—than they had been with us. At Enon, we attended and joined the Enon Baptist Church. It was a small country church, very active, with many dedicated Christians. There were a goodly number of old people who attended this church. They seemed to have a special love and understanding for young people. Then, there were a number of "not so old people" who provided lots of activities for young people. We put on programs for special days, we attended roasts, ice cream socials, we went on hayrides, and numerous other activities. I think this was the very happiest time of my young life. We had a wonderful song leader, and had "singing schools" about every year. At singing school, we learned the music to new songs and would have special music at church services from the songs. Many of these "not so old" people had a significant influence on my life during this time. They all were "terrific", and I loved and respected all of them. I thought many of them fit the description of "saint"—their faces shining with the glory of God when they stood up to testify of His goodness.

Music for the songs was written in shape notes. Each note of the scale had its own distinctive shape. This was fine for singing school, but once one became dependent on reading music this way, it seemed more difficult to read the normal round notes in music class or Glee Club in high school.

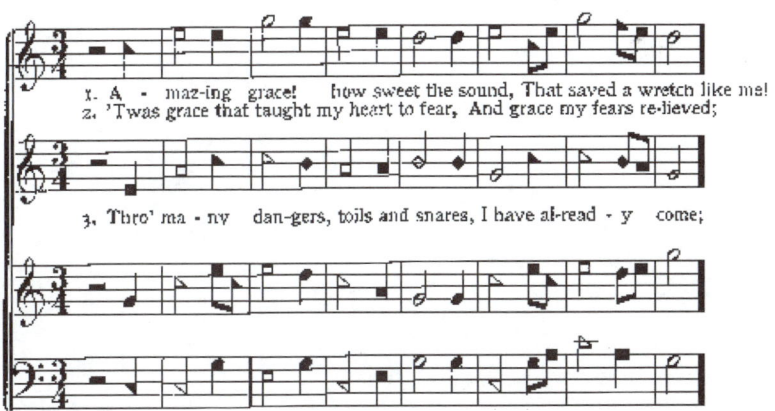

Photograph 13 An illustration of Shape-notes from <u>The Original Sacred Harp</u>, which is a shape-note hymnal first published in 1844 by Benjamin Franklin White and in print continuously since then, last revised in 1991.

47

Chapter Five
High School

I started attending Nicholas County High School in Summersville in 1920. Mom and Pop had moved to Enon for the express purpose of getting us within walking distance to Summersville. Walking distance was about three miles, or the better part of an hour each way. The norm in those days was to finish eighth grade and then go to work. To some degree, going on to high school was the equivalent of going on to college today: available mostly for the better students, and for the wealthier families.

It should be remembered that we were poor, relatively speaking, and high school was expensive. It was expensive because we needed to purchase books, clothes, and lunches. Additionally, it was necessary for Mom to arrange for an emergency place for us to stay in the event of inclement weather. She had arranged for us to stay overnight with the janitor and his wife who routinely took in student boarders in any case. Also, going to high school represented loss-of-income since many children of high school age were already in the work force. For this reason, many of my fellow students were up in their twenties or thirties, having come back to finish high school after some years of employment.

About the time I started high school, the last of my siblings was born. On September 3, 1920, Robert Warren joined the family. Because of the age difference, I was 14 years older than Warren, and he seemed almost like a son or nephew to me. Much later in life, he would live with Don and me, and indeed he was like a son. The boys were all very mischievous, but Warren more so than the other two.

Luke was the most tenderhearted. All my siblings were inventive and all grew up to be fine women and men.

Enon stands out as one of my favorite places compared to all the many places we lived. To that point, Mom and Pop had never owned a home, but always rented. Enon was no exception, and I suspect this was as close to Summersville as they could afford, as rentals generally got more expensive the closer to town they were.

The road to Summersville was unpaved which was bad enough, but while we were in high school they paved it. That meant for at least a year it was worked-up mud, and a miserable walk. I said that it took the better part of one hour to walk the three miles, but that was not a constant. The first year, at least for a few months, Bert and I walked it rather briskly. One of the little incidents I remember on the walk was Bert and I arguing over who would carry the lunch. With what I viewed as obstinacy on her part, and no hope for a satisfactory accommodation, I simply tossed the lunch over the bank along side the road. I learned my lesson well when I suffered greatly at lunchtime, and all afternoon for that matter.

We were very apprehensive of getting "tardy marks", because such marks equated to an absence, and we cared, since absences affected your grade. Bert left school to attend Alderson Academy, and I continued to walk briskly, and had no problem with tardiness. When I was a junior, Vern started high school, and for some reason, she couldn't keep the pace, so we compensated by starting earlier, something I didn't relish.

I remember the building from three-quarters of a century ago as a cut-stone, three-story building, that was very impressive, if not beautiful. It was so well constructed that

Photograph 14 NCHS in 1923 looks very much like it does today. The building is used today for county offices

it is still in use as a county office building. The current Nicholas County High School has a site on the Internet, and the site pictures a beautiful modern brick building. This was my first experience of changing rooms, and changing classes, with each period of study. Of course, as is the freshman tradition, I got lost much to my chagrin. I remember the lights in the school were very good. They were not the customary kerosene lamps we had in homes of that era. They might have been carbide, or natural gas lamps, or even early electric lights, as not long after this a few "well-off" homeowners had "Delco" generator/battery electric light systems in their homes.

Like most students at one time or another, I had a crush on my history teacher. I really thought he was handsome, and, needless to say, history was my favorite subject, and one in which I particularly excelled. Looking back, he was a rather ordinary looking, if not homely, person.

I started dating Earl Neil in high school, and continued this relationship throughout my years at Nicholas County High School. Earl was well liked by Warren, who was a toddler and could not talk very plain. Warren would confront Earl in a crowded place, such as church, and say "Erdie Needy ooh dot eeny chuggie dum?" (Translation: Earl Neil, do

51

you have any chewing gum?) To which, Earl would produce the gum. Earl was not in school; in fact, as I remember, he did not go to school beyond eighth grade. It seemed like wherever I was, he would appear. This was acceptable in high school, and even somehow desirable, but after I left high school, he would appear at Swiss where I was teaching. I soon tired of this smothering, and broke the relationship off rather bluntly.

Maynie Morriston, as I mentioned earlier, was one of my better friends in high school. Maynie boarded at the janitor's home, our emergency overnight foul-weather refuge. I had known Maynie from Zela, and we remained friends for life. There were other special friends in high school; Agnes Walker was one of them. I remember Agnes as one of those people who always had something interesting to tell, usually something very funny.

Photograph 15   Maynie Morriston's picture from our NCHS Junior Year-book

My first date was with the preacher's son. I was 14, and he was 15. He tried to get me to kiss him, so I told him I did not want to go out with him anymore. He had walked me home from church on Saturday night. The next day, there was a baptizing in the creek near the church. His mother came over to me and said, "Somebody was just about killed last night." Red faced and terribly embarrassed, I didn't even answer, but quickly mingled in the crowd to get away from her. Most of our dates centered on church activities. Boys walked their girls home from church. They would line up at the door of the church, and as the girls came out they would ask if they could walk them home. Many courtships started this way. If everything were congenial, the boy would ask if he could come and get the girl and bring her to church, or some other activity, and of course bring her back home.

Boys also came to the house to see the girls of their choice. The preacher's wife later informed me that I had broken her son's heart because I wouldn't be his girlfriend.

I remember a boy named Van Dorsey, who was to become Superintendent of Raleigh County Schools, and therefore, my boss in later years. However, the Van that I knew could not do math at all, and only survived by using my problem solutions. I remember a cruel trick that Van played on his rather naïve sister Minnie (see page from yearbook for pictures of Minnie and Van). We were supposed to tell an anecdote to illustrate the use of the term. Van told her the following "There was a dog who chased a car, the car ran over its tail cutting off the end of it and making the dog angry, so he kept chasing the car until it ran over his head. The moral of this story is: don't lose your head over a little piece of tail." Minnie innocently read this anecdote before the class, much to her shock, when the "other" meaning was explained to her.

Another special friend was Camille Cavendish, who was also a bit of a prankster, often at my expense. One incident involved a promising young man, named

Photograph 16 Leonard Strickland from our Junior Class yearbook

53

Leonard Strickland, who was later to become a highly respected doctor. I had no interest in Leonard, who was somewhat short and stocky, and today would be regarded

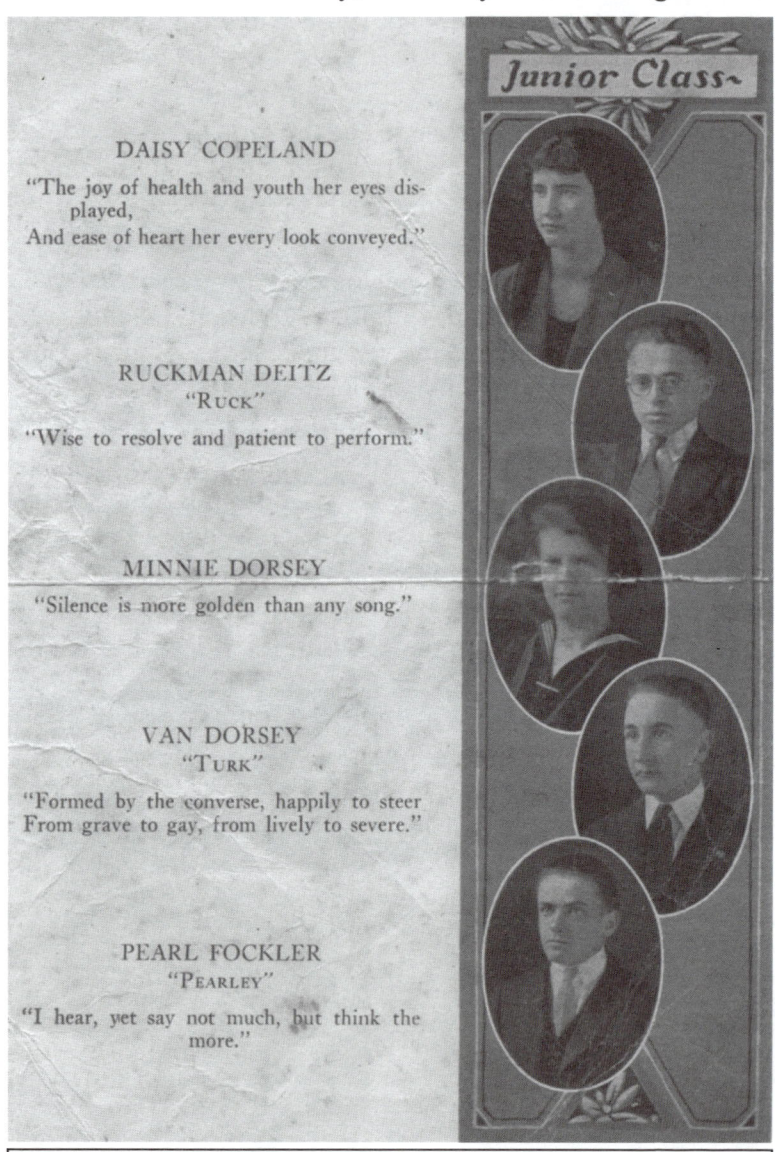

Junior Class

DAISY COPELAND

"The joy of health and youth her eyes displayed,
And ease of heart her every look conveyed."

RUCKMAN DEITZ
"RUCK"

"Wise to resolve and patient to perform."

MINNIE DORSEY

"Silence is more golden than any song."

VAN DORSEY
"TURK"

"Formed by the converse, happily to steer
From grave to gay, from lively to severe."

PEARL FOCKLER
"PEARLEY"

"I hear, yet say not much, but think the more."

Photograph 17 My page in the 1923 (Junior year) NCHS yearbook. (Note Minnie and Van Dorsey.)

as somewhat of a "nerd". Camille, with some co-conspirators, wrote me a letter, supposedly from him, which asked for a date. I was very angry, and labored over how to respond, and was on the verge of sending a very unkind, blunt refusal, when they came clean. Ironically, Leonard actually asked me for a date some time later, which I refused, more kindly than I had in my never-sent letter.

There were regional competitions in speeches and essays, and probably other scholarly skills. A winner from each high school would represent the school in a county-wide competition. The competition in Nicholas County was between our school and Richwood High School, since they were the only other high schools in the county. The county winner would then represent the school in a state-wide competition or a regional competition. I tied with another girl from our school for an essay competition. The winner was decided by drawing straws. The other girl won, and I always suspected they mercifully let her win because I would not have had the appropriate clothes to wear to such a prestigious event.

I remember whispering with my friends in study hall. When the teacher caught us, and we were told to stop it, I wrote a note saying something to the effect "We can't whisper, but we can pass notes". This teacher was on the ball, and saw me passing the note; whereupon, I was required to come to the front of the room and read the note. Another lesson well learned, and a discipline technique noted that I later employed as a teacher.

Despite the occasional lesson learned the hard way, I did quite well in high school. For better students, there was an opportunity to earn college credits by taking extra courses. I actually left high school with 8-10 college credits, which I used toward my teaching certificate, and ultimately toward my college degree. These credits represented the equivalent of one summer in college, and since I spent so many of my summers over the next quarter-century working toward my degree, perhaps sometime those hours were one summer of freedom from the books. As I recall, these college-credit courses were in literature or sociology.

My parents worked hard, sacrificed and did without things for themselves to make sure I got through high school. My sister, Bertha, quit high school after her sophomore year and taught school two years to help pay for Vern's and my schooling. After I graduated from high school, I taught school so she and Vernice could finish high school. With my college credit from high school, I attended summer school enough to earn what was known as Short Course Normal Certificate. After I married, I went to college taking courses at night, Saturdays, and attending summer school, until I finally earned my BS Degree in Education in 1950. Throughout this time, I had the help and encouragement of my parents, my siblings, my husband, and my children. Bert stayed at my house in the summer, and we drove to school. We had several classes together so she helped me by going over her notes with me while I drove. I don't know how I would have ever passed the courses without her help, because I had so much work to do at home.

About the time when I was in high school, many people including my dad, bought Model T Ford cars. No one was required to have driver's license. My dad bought his car, and drove it home without having any training in driving. I also bought a car when I started teaching. I left it at home when I went to Oak Hill to teach. I allowed Vernice to drive it to summer school, but was secretly irritated when I heard her referring to the car as "my car."

Chapter Six
A Career Begins

In the spring of 1924, I graduated from high school and
began my teaching career at Swiss in a three-room school,
not the school I had attended as a child when we lived in
Swiss. The staff consisted of a principal, who also taught,
another beginning teacher, Marie Longacre, and me. My
job was first, second, and third grades. I specifically
remember two of the children, both very bright, and both
very pretty, but also very different. Olive Burdette was a
small child with dark eyes and dark hair cut short with
bangs. Pansy Brown was also very pretty, but she had a
light complexion with sandy hair, and always wore her hair
in braids.

It was too far from Enon to Swiss for me to commute. In
fact, the distance even prohibited visits home except on
holidays. I boarded at the home of the Forsythe family. I
don't remember them well, but there were children, and
Mr. Forsythe managed the company store. Mrs. Forsythe
also provided board for the circuit rider preachers who
served the Swiss churches. The only time I specifically
remember going home was at Christmas, when Earl Neil
borrowed a team of horses, and brought me home.

At Swiss, I started dating a boy named James Wright.
James was a good, hard-working person who took care of
his mother and siblings, because his father was dead. After
I returned from Swiss, James wrote a letter every day much
to Mom's chagrin.

I got the job at Swiss probably because the trustees came to
the high school, and I had some college credits. I don't
remember how much I earned, but it was Mom and Pop's
expectation that after I paid my board and bought some

clothes, that whatever was left over would go toward the family budget. There were other children to put through high school, and as I indicated earlier, high school was expensive. The family moved to Hookersville on Muddlety River during the year I was away.

The next two years, I taught at a one-room school up the Muddlety River. At Hookersville, there was a small one-room school right across the road from home. This was ideal, considering the long distance to my last school in Swiss. It was not to be. Mr. Charlie McQueen was the trustee who was hiring for the Muddlety schools, and he placed me in a school that was three miles away. I took the job, but coveted that nearby school, as I walked to and from work each day.

After one year, Vern graduated from high school, took some college credits in the summer, and was available for teaching during my second year. She accepted a school two miles further from home than mine. Both schools were in the same direction, so we walked the three miles together. The disgust about our not being able to get the nearby school ultimately led to our leaving the county. To make it even more puzzling, Mr. McQueen was active in the church, as were Vern and I, so we had considerable contact with him, and felt he could give us no reasonable explanation for not assigning one of us to the school across the road.

While we were teaching at Muddlety, I bought restaurant furniture, and Pop closed off a back porch on the house, and created a lunchroom from part of the house. The furniture was like that commonly used in an ice cream parlor, wrought iron tables and chairs. Mom did the cooking, and she prepared wonderful meals. She also made wonderful ham sandwiches on homemade loaves of bread or biscuits. They may have been too elaborate or too expensive for the paltry sum we asked for them, because we never made any money, and soon closed shop.

Bert and I met surveyors at this lunchroom. Bert was stuck on one named Carver, and I started dating one named Gay Jones. I fell in love with him, and he kept talking about going back to Ivydale to get a ring. When the job was finished, he left, and that was the last of him. This served me right, because I had done Earl Neil kind of dirty, and had broken his heart. Earl was the type that was moody, and his family blamed me because he started drinking. His parents were dead, and he lived with his Uncle Charlie Neil. His sister would write to Vern blaming me for his problems. After I married, she wrote a letter to Vern wanting me to date him. Vern got the letter, and wrote telling him I was married and had a baby.

After my second year at Muddlety, Bert and I were in summer school, living with Aunt Bert (Mom's sister) in Oak Hill, taking classes for a teaching certificate, and by chance met a boy named Brookes. He told us about a place called Peachtree, in Raleigh County, that had openings for teachers. The situation at Muddlety, where Vern and I had schools and had to walk 3-5 miles to teach, had us looking; and, besides, Mom's brother Jubal Hurt (Uncle Jube) was very familiar with the Peachtree area, and could pave the way for us.

In the fall of 1927, I took a job teaching on Peachtree Creek, a tributary of Marsh Fork of Big Coal River, in Raleigh County. Uncle Jube was familiar with the area because he was a nurseryman who sold trees, plants and seeds throughout the neighboring counties. He made the necessary arrangements including contacting the school trustees, and finding a nice place for us to board. Mr.

59

Charlie Pettry, who was a school trustee, hired me for one of the tiny rural schools on Peachtree Creek, and Bert for a second school. However, at the last moment, Bert declined to go because she was happy with her position at Blakely School in Nicholas County, and I brought Vern with me as a substitute. I suppose because it was time for school to start, Mr. Pettry accepted her without a fuss. He certainly was aware of the switch, because years later he would laugh about how I had switched sisters on him.

We boarded at the home of King Webb and his wife Citie. They were a kindly couple who had four children. Their daughter, Elsie May, married Andrew Bonds, and had two children who often visited the family. There was a second daughter Sylvia, who was about our age, and two sons, Dale and Kermit, who were considerably younger than we were. Dale (age 6) claimed me as his sweetheart, while Kermit (age 3) said he got the big one (Vern). Mrs. Webb had a parlor, which was available to us for entertaining. Frequently, several young people would simply congregate there for a social gathering without specifically having a date.

Photograph 18 Dale Webb and I

Photograph 19 Vernice and I, c. 1927.

The Webbs were the most industrious people I have ever known. The day started very early for the whole family, with Citie and Sylvia quilting constantly, adding to the huge stack of quilts they had already made. I am sure they sold them, as there were far too many for any family to use. King raised a big garden, selling some of the produce, and the remainder was canned for their use. Apples and berries were sold, along with the produce, to the miners in the coal camps. They raised and sold chickens, hogs, and cattle. Citie made the best stack cakes, which still make my mouth water as I think of them. She would put slices in the lunch boxes she prepared for us. A stack cake was sweetened with molasses, and then rolled until it was nearly as thin as a pancake. Citie flavored her batter with a little bit of vanilla. She would stack about eight layers to a stack with spicy cooked apples layered between cakes.

A very sad thing happened soon after we arrived at King and Citie Webb's. A neighbor of theirs, and perhaps a relative, Crockett Webb, had two small boys who became ill with diphtheria. They had been ill several days, and were in the same bed, when one of the boys died. The other little boy saw him die, became frightened, and got up and ran. He got to the door of the room, and dropped dead himself. Vern and I were so sad about this, and we felt so sorry for the family, that we wanted to do something to help. We wanted to go and wash the little boys for burial. Citie was very much against us going, because she was afraid that we would get diphtheria ourselves, or bring it back to her family. She finally agreed that we could do it, but only on the condition, that we bathe ourselves, and change into different clothes before we came back to her house. I think she made us burn the clothes we wore to do the bathing.

Chapter Seven
A Family Begins

Photograph 20 Don and I before we were married.

I met Don Jarrell for the first time when a group of young men were going to a fire tower to spend the night. They passed by the house where Vernice and I were boarding. Their group was in a big truck, a number of them standing in the bed of the truck. The group whistled and cheered as they passed the house where Vern, Sylvia, and I were standing. I don't think I saw any of the group except Don. Sometime later, I had a date with his friend, a fellow named Luther Miller, and Vern had a date with Don. I had thought Don was the finest looking man I had ever seen. He was tall, broad shouldered, with light brown hair and blue eyes. Apparently he thought well of me also, because, before the night was over, Don asked me if he could take me to church, and of course, I agreed. That was my first date with him.

We dated the rest of the year from the time we met, which was only a few days after we got there at our boarding house. Don asked me to marry him not long before school was out in April. I said, "yes!!" When the school term ended, Don took Vern and me home to meet my parents and the rest of the family. About two weeks later, he came back after me, and we were married May 5, 1928. He brought his brother, Hobert, with him to act as a witness at out wedding. My parents could not afford to pay for a wedding for me, so we stopped in Beckley, and were married on our way back to his home. We had gotten the marriage license in Summersville; therefore the marriage was registered in Nicholas county, the home county of the bride, as was required. Nearly sixty years later, just after Don's death, I needed proof of our marriage to settle the estate, and went to Beckley, the county seat of Raleigh County only to find no record existed. After a few moments of bewilderment, I remembered that even though we were married in Raleigh County, it would have been recorded in Nicholas County, so a trip to Summersville proved it was legal after all.

Here is the way I described our wedding to Mom and Pop.

Written by Daisy Copeland Jarrell, Tuesday, May 8, 1928

Pineknob, W. Va.
May 8,1928

Dear Mamma, Papa and all the folks,

I guess I must tell you some of the trials of getting married. We got our license in Summersville. We were so excited that neither of us could hardly write our names. We didn't get half so excited when we got married. We were married in Beckley at about four o'clock Saturday. Then we came on to the Jarrells. Lots of Don's relatives were here and they had the best supper. People were just lined up from one end of the creek to another to serenade us, but Don's grandmother fell and hurt her leg so no one came, but they nearly set us crazy the next night serenading us.

My picture was in Beckley sure enough. That studio was doing some work for the Oak Hill Studio for advertisement and my picture was sent with some others.

Vern, Hobert, and I are coming Monday. I think Ruby and her beau are coming, too. So expect us all Monday for supper.

Love /Daisy/

Photograph 21 This picture of Don and me was taken some time after our wedding.

Our wedding day was a beautiful day, but I was so nervous I could hardly write when we stopped at the courthouse to get our marriage license. From there, we went on to Beckley, and were married in the Methodist parsonage by the minister there. Vernice and Hobert were our witnesses. From there, we went on to Don's home. I think the whole community was planning on giving us a "belling", a big serenade, in which people rang bells or beat on kettles or anything that made noise. This went on until the bride and groom "treated" the crowd with candy or some kind of refreshments. Unfortunately, Don's grandmother, Victoria Jarrell Pettry, fell as she was coming down the steps of Don's father's house and broke her hip, so we escaped this ceremony. Those serenades sometimes became pretty wild, with people putting the couple in a wheelbarrow and taking them for a ride. Sometimes they rode the groom on a rail. I did not have a mother-in-law, because Don's mother had died, and was buried about the time I came to Pineknob to teach.

Photograph 22 The picture that Don saw in a photography shop in Beckley.

The picture I mentioned in the letter was one that Don had seen in a photographer's window. He had tried to buy it, but the photographer asked if he was related, and Don said no, at which time the photographer refused to sell it to him. We told him that being a fiancé is probably close enough kin to have answered in the affirmative. We later went back together and bought the picture.

Don was one of the most unselfish people I ever saw. His family always came first. He was an excellent host, so thoughtful and considerate. He was always very good to my parents and my siblings. People in the community always knew they could depend on him to help if they couldn't start their cars, or needed to be pulled out of a ditch. He never refused to loan tools to people, although many tools were never returned. He was my "burden-bearer". Whatever the problem, he always had a solution. He didn't always remember my birthday, or our anniversary, but showed his love in so many other ways, that I didn't mind.

The following fall I started teaching in Packsville, another small school at the head of another hollow. We lived in a coal company house, (a two-family house which would now be called a duplex), at Eunice. There our first child, Phyllis, was born on March 16th of the following year, 1929. In that two family house, another family lived with a toddler. She was a cute little girl, but she had a habit of just walking into our half of the house. Don was somewhat bothered about this, but her parents seemed unconcerned. Don fixed this by giving her a straight razor, which she promptly took home to her mother. Needless to say, we didn't see her unaccompanied anymore.

Photograph 23 Don and I with Phyllis and our 1929 Roadster.

67

In the fall of that year, the Great Depression began with a vengeance, and Pop wanted Don to come to Nicholas County, where he was sure he could find work in the lumber business. Don did find some work, but wages were poor, and we just couldn't make it on the wages he was paid. I was pregnant with our second child, and Don decided it would be better for him to return to Eunice to the coal mines where wages were meager, but better than what he was getting in Nicholas County.

Mom thought it would not be suitable for me to return to Raleigh County with Don until after the baby was born. Donald Winfield arrived on November 23, 1930, with his father still away from home working in Raleigh County. When Don came for Christmas, he brought a pretty tricycle for Phyllis, but nothing for Donald. I thought this was terrible; of course, Donald was only a month old and could not have cared less. When this story was told years later, the other children would always joke that this oversight scarred Donald for life.

While I was in Nicholas County awaiting Donald's arrival, Don and his dad were building a little house for us on a plot of land his mother had given to him. Despite Mom's warning that the house would be too cold for us to take two babies into, I returned to Coal River with Don when Donald was six-weeks old. Much to my chagrin, Mom was right. The little cheaply-built house was not a good place for babies. The rest of the winter was pretty bad with Phyllis and Donald coughing and sick most of the time. We got a baby sitter to stay all of the time with us in the house, and I taught at Birchton for six weeks for a teacher, Chessie Bennet, who had broken her leg. This came in handy years later; when I applied for retirement, I got credit for this six-weeks of teaching. The six-weeks was very difficult because we had an old truck, which constantly stayed broken down, and Don was afraid for me to drive it alone. Lowell came and stayed with us to drive me to and from school.

The mines were shutting down because of the depression, and Don worked on the county roads for a dollar a day. I got a full-time job teaching, but teachers' pay was deferred for months at a time. We were paid, but never knew when it would come. Faye came to stay and look after Phyllis, Donald, and a new baby, Betty.

Once, during the depression, Don's dad came and handed him $20, and I don't think $20 ever looked so good as it did then. I am sure Mr. Jarrell did not have money to spare, and

Photograph 24 Phyllis standing in front of the little house and the old truck.

he had a reputation for being tight-fisted, but this act of kindness profoundly influenced my opinion of him from then forward. I remember one thing Don did with part of the money was to buy a big sack of beans. I am sure they didn't cost very much, because I remember bread costing ten cents a loaf. That sack of beans was the main course in most of our suppers over the following months.

Many decades later, one of Minnie's granddaughters met an elderly man in the hospital where she worked. Somehow he found out she was a descendant of Don's dad and her great-grandfather Samuel "Coon" Jarrell. This gentleman indicated that Mr. Jarrell was responsible for the survival of many people in those terrible times, so his "tight-fisted" reputation may not have applied when the chips were down.

We had beans at nearly every evening meal during those hard times. I remember once, probably in the late 1930s when Jerry was four or five years old, he objected when we didn't have pinto beans for dinner. I told him that if he didn't like what we were having, to go to Minnie's house for dinner. He did, and she had beans, so he returned after dinner quite pleased with himself. I was reminded by the girls that this wasn't the first time he had demanded beans for dinner. On earlier occasions, I had sent them to Minnie's house to get beans. I suppose I let him get away with this because he was a finicky eater, and very skinny, so I was desperate to get him to eat.

Photograph 25 Don, c. 1928.

Don: As I have said, when I first met Don in 1927, I thought he was the most handsome man I had ever seen. He was tall and strong, and yet, he seemed gentle and caring. Don was not an educated man, yet he had a kind of self-taught wisdom that few people seem to have. His formal education stopped at around the third grade. He could read well enough, and could write, but his handwriting was poor and labored. Some of that may be attributable to the condition of his hands, as they were frequently injured in mining accidents over the years.

His formal education stopped because he went to work at the age of eight years to drive a team of horses. His real education never stopped, because he read the newspapers all his life, and in his later years, he devoured books. He had a rudimentary understanding of business and finance, but most of all he was a people person. He was gregarious, in that he was around people, and wanted people around him. From that perspective, he was a natural politician. I think if you had asked Don how he wanted to be remembered, he would have said that he wanted to be remembered as an honest man. I don't believe Don ever knowingly cheated anyone out of anything.

Don was impatient with people. The children never moved fast enough to suit him, and he was rough on them. In retrospect, his treatment of the children bordered on mistreatment, but fairly severe punishment was the norm of the day. He trusted the children to independently complete a job, and held them accountable. For this reason, they assumed responsibility at a very young age, particularly the older children.

His impatience with people applied to anyone in the neighborhood whom he judged to be behaving irresponsibly; in particular, he couldn't tolerate public drunkenness. One of the neighbors was particularly bad about getting drunk and causing trouble as he passed by our house on the way to his house. On more than one occasion, Don would confront him, more often than not physically.

On one occasion, this gentleman was throwing rocks at our chickens when Don spotted him, wherewith he took off his belt and whipped him, for perhaps 100 yards up the road,

71

all the while he was yelling, "I'm going Don, I'm sorry!"
Don replied, "But you're not going fast enough."

For some reason, he seemed to dislike certain members of
his mother's family. I got the impression that it had something to do with their lack of support when his mother was
dying. The children noticed he didn't particularly like his
Mom's younger sister, his Aunt Ida. On one occasion, he
lied to avoid seeing her and Phyllis contradicted him in
front of her. He was very upset with Phyllis. He also
looked down on his uncle Clifford Hunter, (formally
DeClifford). In comparison with some of the other family
members who were doctors or dentists, it might have been
that, in his eyes, Clifford just didn't amount to much.
Clifford inherited the home place, and may have been
viewed by Don as an unadventurous "Mama's Boy."
Clifford was the child born after his mother lost two
children to diphtheria in 1875, so he may have been special
to his mother. Don just tolerated him, but didn't associate
with him unnecessarily.

One other incident involving the Hunters comes to mind.
Don's uncle, Charles Hunter, Charley to all of us, occasionally worked as a carpenter, and we used his services
when we added a second story to our house on Drews
Creek. The children knew him fairly well. One day, in
1941, someone came by the house to tell Don that Charley
had died. Don was with Billie and Jerry, and took them
along to check on Charley. When they arrived, they didn't
know quite what to expect. In fact, the children probably
didn't know anything about what had happened. Charley
had committed suicide by running a garden hose from his
automobile's exhaust pipe around through the driver's
window and asphyxiated himself. The children ran over to
the car wide-eyed, and jumped up on the running board
about a foot from his body. They quickly saw the error of

their ways, and retreated to a father who sheepishly realized he had let them go too far.

Don tended to be jealous. My brother Luke in his book describes him as follows: "Don was a good fellow, quite enterprising, and easy going. He did not share Daisy's education and he was always irrationally jealous of her. Nevertheless he was a kind and generous man and they had a strong and enduring marriage." Luke is right about the jealousy, Don was jealous of the men I taught with, and of virtually every man I had any association with. This made things difficult because men, occupying all of the important positions, ran the teaching profession. Don was even jealous of my old boy friends, particularly Earl Neil whom he never met, but heard about from my family. He always thought, perhaps with some justification, that they would have preferred that I marry Earl. He also got into arguments several times with men, nearly fighting over things that happened at school between their kids and me.

He held many jobs, and had a reputation for being a good worker, so he could get a job when they were hard to come by. Most of his years were in the coal mines. He worked his way up to being a motor operator, which means he operated the small electric locomotive that moved coal cars into the mine to be loaded, and out of the mine to be emptied. On the way up, he did the most undesirable jobs, for example, picking slate, which meant looking at the coal, or digging through the coal, to cull out pieces of slate. He also loaded coal, which in the early years literally meant shoveling the coal into the cars. Often this work was done in "low coal", which meant spending the day on his knees, because the ceiling was too low to stand upright. The children remember his carbide lamp, and later electrical lamps, his hard hat, (hard hats such as this were later adapted for use as baseball batting helmets), his lunch bucket, and his coal-blackened face and clothes.

Among the papers left for the family were his pay envelopes for his work for Princess Dorothy Coal Company at Eunice during the period October 15, 1942, through December 18, 1948, and for his work for Raleigh Wyoming Mining Company at Edwight during the period January 15, 1957 through February 15, 1958.

These pay envelopes provide an interesting look at the hours of work for persons on the "home front" during World War II (December 8, 1941, to September 2, 1945.) During this period, many persons worked long hours as their contribution to the war effort, as well as for the extra pay.

It appears, from these records, that miners working under United Mine Workers of America contract (all the mines Don worked for during this period were under union contract) received 1.5 times their regular hourly pay rate for all hours worked over 7 hours in a day or 40 hours in a week   Don typically worked as many hours overtime as hours worked at "straight" time during this wartime period. During this time, he worked an average of 146 hours a month at regular pay, and 157 hours at overtime pay, for a combined total of 303 hours per month. Assuming a 6-day workweek, this would average out to over 11 1/2 hours a day. The fewest hours worked in a month during this period was 163, in January 1943, and the maximum, worked in May 1944, was 391 hours. This latter figure averages out to 15 hours per day, assuming, again, that he worked a 6-day workweek (27 days in May 1944).

Many of the overtime hours Don worked were spent driving the miners' bus to haul miners to and from work.

Because it was difficult to buy gasoline and tires for privately owned vehicles during the war, the coal company had to provide a bus to get the employees to work. Don drove a bus in and out of Peachtree hauling miners who lived on Drews Creek and Peachtree and also picking up riders at various places along Route 3.

The pay envelopes also illustrate Don's willingness to work overtime when offered the opportunity. Even during the peacetime year of work in 1957-1958, he averaged about 7 1/2 hours of overtime a month. Don was not unusual in his willingness to work overtime. Coal miners knew that the mines could not be counted on for regular employment so they tended to work overtime when it was offered to them to get something ahead for the times without work. But the overtime work had to be needed and offered by the company, so the amount of overtime worked was not primarily at the discretion of the employee. Even so, Don was probably somewhat unusual in the amount of overtime he worked for two reasons. First, for much of his mining career he worked at jobs that allowed more opportunity to work overtime.

When he worked at Eunice during the wartime period, he worked most of this time as a motorman, and overtime was frequently available to him. And, as mentioned above, he drove the miners' bus before and after his regular shift of work and received overtime pay for this work. However, when he returned to the mines in 1957, he returned, without seniority, to Raleigh Wyoming Mining Company at Edwight. He had to begin at lower-ranked jobs such as track cleaner and inside laborer, and worked little overtime (an average of 3 hours per month) on these jobs. Later, when he occasionally worked at the top of the occupational ladder, as motorman, he worked on average 17 hours of overtime each pay period.

A second reason Don was able to work overtime while in the coal mines, was that he had the reputation of being a dependable and hard worker. This translated into his favorable treatment in the assignment of overtime. This reputation also allowed Don to get second jobs with other employers, which he frequently did, for example as night watchman, in addition to his regular full-time job. And it was this aspect of his work of which Don was most proud, his reputation as a good worker. When he talked about his work, he most frequently talked about his ability to get another job when he lost his job as a result of a layoff or closing of a mine. He seemed always to have another job waiting at another mine so that he would go from the one job almost directly to the next one.

This also is a testimonial to the fact that he was an exceptionally ingenious and dedicated employee. His employers tried on occasion to get him to go into management, but he never wanted to go in that direction. (Few miners did, for they realized how difficult it was to leave the union ranks and go into management.) Don probably lost many of the contacts he had developed during his early years in the mines when he left the mines to become deputy sheriff, but he was able to say until then that he was never out of a job for more than a day.

The great fears of the coalmines were two-fold, a ceiling cave-in or an explosion. There were not many explosions around the mines Don worked in, perhaps the methane buildup was not particularly a problem there, but there were cave-ins. The most common type of cave-in was referred to as a "slate fall", where the slate layer overlaying the working coalface of the mine would collapse.

In the mid-1930's, Don was badly injured in such a slate fall. His chest and face were crushed, and when he arrived

76

at the hospital, he was pretty much written off. He was left on a Gurney in a hallway, and was not being treated. By chance or divine providence, his uncle, Robert Hunter, a physician, happened by and recognized him either by his appearance or by his name. At any rate, Dr. Hunter, insisted that he get immediate care, and he recovered. He always credited Dr. Hunter for saving his life. While there were members of his mother's family he didn't seem to respect, Robert Hunter was certainly an exception. In other mine accidents he suffered a broken nose more than once, and suffered broken ribs, hands and fingers on several occasions.

He also drove a school bus for several years, and was a real favorite among the teens in the community. He had a great rapport with young people, often teasing them incessantly.

His happiest days at work probably were as deputy sheriff. His grandfather had been Raleigh County Sheriff, and Deputy Sheriff so, to some degree, he was following in Lewis Hunter's footsteps. This was an elective office where each candidate for sheriff was on the ballot with an understood slate of deputies, each representing a district of the county. He was extremely good at electioneering, but he was not a public speaker. His forte was one-on-one persuasion. He was generally good at this type of work, with enough education to handle the paperwork. Later the deputies had to be high school graduates and more recently college graduates. The disadvantage to this work was that the sheriff had to stand for election every four years, so you could never be sure you would be employed after the next election.

Probably the job he liked next most was state road foreman for Marsh Fork District. This came after his sheriff candidate was defeated for election by a candidate with a slate replacing Don with his nephew Edgar Jarrell. Don was a natural at the road job, and had all of the pent-up irritation with the roads from his years of traveling them as deputy sheriff. He was enough of a practical engineer to know how to fix things, and to know why the road surface broke down. He also knew where the political sensitivities were so that the squeaky wheel was greased.

For a short while at Drews Creek, and again in his retirement years at Naoma, he ran a country store. Again, his people skills were invaluable to him. He loved to spend his time around the coal heater in the store, exchanging stories with customers and friends. His wide array of experiences, and his acute interest in almost everything, gave him a vast storehouse of material to draw from. Additionally, by this time, his children and sons- and daughters-in-law also provided bragging material. During this time, he was active in fishing and hunting, and had a string of friends with similar interests. He also was a die-hard fan of the Philadelphia Phillies, so he could selectively debate the local fans who were mostly devotees of the Atlanta Braves or the Cincinnati Reds.

The Children: We had six children, four girls, and two boys. I will simply list the children by name, with a short biographical sentence or two on each. Anecdotal evidence as to their wit and character is presented in other parts of this book.

Photograph 26 Phyllis c. 1938.

Phyllis Jean was born March 16, 1929, at Eunice, in Raleigh County, our only pre-depression baby. She was born in a coal company house and she was delivered by the company doctor. She married Ralph Aquino of Brooklyn, New York, in 1951. They were both teachers, now retired.

They have four children and ten grandchildren. Phyllis and Ralph live in Chillicothe, Ohio. Phyllis was extremely precious to us, and we probably started off spoiling her; however, she wasn't the baby very long.

Photograph 27 The children and me with Nell Cox (Don's niece) in 1941. (L-R, front: Betty, Jerry, Billie, back: Phyllis, me holding Garnet, Nell and Donald.)

Our first son joined us about 20 months later. Don and I had left Raleigh County, in search of a better paying job, and were living with my parents at Hookersville, in Nicholas County, while I was pregnant with Donald. Don was unhappy with the wages he could earn in the lumber industry there, and we decided he should go back to Raleigh County and find a job and build us a house. He took care of both of these chores, but Mom persuaded me to stay there until the baby was born so there would be help with Phyllis. On November 23, 1930, Donald Winfield arrived, with the distinction of being the only one of the children not born in Raleigh County. When Donald was six-weeks old, we took the children and moved back to Raleigh County. Just after Christmas, 1930, we moved into "our" first house.

Photograph 28 Donald, c. 1938.

Donald married Joanne Straley of New Cumberland, Pennsylvania, in 1957. Donald earned a bachelors degree in mining engineering, and later earned a masters degree and a doctorate in economics from The University of Pennsylvania, and was a professor at Drexel University in Philadelphia, now retired. Joanne is a former secondary and college teacher. They have two children. Donald and Joanne live in Valley Forge, Pennsylvania.

Betty Lois joined our growing family at Drews Creek, back in Raleigh County. Betty was the only child born in the "new" house that Don had built before it was burned.

Photograph 29 Betty, c. 1938.

Betty Lois was born April 12, 1932 at Pineknob, in Raleigh County. She married Kelton Pennington of Princeton, West Virginia in 1953. Betty was a teacher for 31 years, now retired. Kelton was a Chemist for 33 years prior to his death in 1993. They had four children and four grandchildren. One child, Nancy, died in infancy in 1956. As widows, Betty and I lived together in Polk City, Florida, after 1994. I suspect that without this period together, I might never have appreciated just what a wonderful, giving person Betty is. She truly has been a blessing to me, far beyond my wildest dreams.

A year and a half after Betty's arrival, and after another "new" house was built, our third daughter joined the family. Billie Lou was born September 26, 1933, also at Pineknob. Billie was known for her fear of nothing. One story involving Billie must be told here. Don, and at least two of the other children, were abnormally afraid of heights. After the new house had been remodeled, it had a sharply pitched roof with a gabled end that was about thirty feet high. Most of the kids would not climb this new roof, and Don climbed it only reluctantly when required. On one occasion, Don and I were returning to the house from the garden, when we looked up and saw five-year old Billie perched on the very top of the roof, with her feet hanging over the gabled end, and gleefully waving to us. We were afraid to speak harshly to her for fear of making her fall, so we made up some sort of story to get her to come down, to see what we had, or something of the sort. She just jumped up, and climbed down the roof, like a roofer, went through the window, and came running down to meet us. At that point she was sternly lectured about the dangers of high places, and perhaps spanked and/or hugged all at the same time.

Photograph 30
Billie, c. 1938.

Billie married Kyle Bailey of Princeton, West Virginia, in 1954. Billie was a teacher and school system administrator, now retired. Kyle is retired from a manufacturing plant. They have one child and five grandchildren. They live in Princeton,

West Virginia, but spend their winters near us in Polk City.

Because I had so many small children, Mom wanted to keep Betty for a while until Billie was a little older. How long Betty stayed with Mom has long been the subject of debate. I contend she stayed for about one year, which would mean she returned when she was about three years old. Betty's memory is considerably different, and suggests she stayed on until she was five or six, and that in fact, she started school in Nicholas County. Luke, in his book, agrees with me, but there is fairly compelling evidence, the memory of the other children for example, and her remembering her specific first-grade teacher in Nicholas County that support Betty's version of the story.

Our second son, Jerry Dean, was born on November 21, 1934, like Billie, and Garnet to come later, he was born in the family home at Drews Creek. His birth, and the continuing heavy workload, might also provide rationale for why Betty might have been allowed to stay on longer at Mom & Pop's place.

Photograph 31 Jerry, c. 1938.

Jerry married Lois Fay Seacrist of Clear Creek, West Virginia, in 1957. Jerry was a teacher, a career naval officer, and a meteorologist. He retired in 2000 as Director of the National Hurricane Center in Miami, Florida. Fay is a homemaker and full time caregiver for their handicapped son, Thomas. They have five children and ten grandchildren. Jerry, Fay and Tom live in Salinas, California, but spend their winters near us in Polk City.

There was a break in the population explosion after Jerry. It was not for another five years, on November 12, 1939, that our final child, Garnet Elaine, was born. Garnet was special because she was at home with us for some years after all the others had left, and even after she married, she lived close enough to visit often, while most of the others lived at considerable distance outside the state. She was the only one left in the nest when we moved from Drews Creek.

Photograph 32 Garnet, c. 1946.

Garnet married Curtis Given of Charleston, West Virginia in 1962. Garnet was the director of a medical laboratory, now retired. Curtis was an electrical contractor, now retired. They have two children and two grandchildren. Garnet and Curtis live full time near us in Polk City.

We had six children, eighteen grandchildren, and thirty great-grandchildren. (Ed. note, one great-grandson, Tanner Given, was born after Mom's death.)

Probably our greatest source of pride was in the fact that all six children finished college, at least to a baccalaureate degree. This was particularly difficult because three were in school at the same time for several years, but we were frugal, and were able to scrape through. Of course, sending them to state-supported schools helped. All of them attended Concord College. Donald graduated from West Virginia University, majoring in mining engineering after taking two years of pre-engineering at Concord. Several earned advance degrees on their own later at various colleges or universities.

The Jarrell Family: Don's parents were Samuel Edward Jarrell and Mary Etta Hunter, parents of twelve children, of which Don was the sixth. I knew Samuel quite well since he was basically our next-door neighbor for twenty years. I never knew Don's mother, Mary Etta Hunter Jarrell. On the day Vernice and I first arrived at Peachtree Creek in Raleigh County to teach in 1927, there was a funeral being held. Don's mother died about that time and we surmised later that it might have been her funeral because it would have occurred about the date we arrived. I first met Don a short time later.

Photograph 33
Samuel Edward
Jarrell

Don's family is probably at least as interesting as the Hurt family. His surname, Jarrell, comes down to his father, Samuel Edward Jarrell, through Samuel's mother, Victoria Jarrell, who was a second (concurrent) wife of a Mormon, Jacob Pettry. Jacob Pettry was really Jacob William Pettry, son of Jacob Pettry. His mother was Celia Gore Pettry, who shares a common ancestry with Senator Albert Gore and Vice President Al Gore. Victoria was the daughter of Frances "Peachy" Jarrell, also without benefit of a husband to provide a surname. Of Peachy's three children, one, James Jarrell, was known to have been a medical doctor. The mother of Peachy was Sarah Pettry Jarrell, wife of Gibson Jarrell, and the sister of

Photograph 34 Don;s grandmother Victoria Jarrell Pettry
with her brother Dr. James
Jarrell (from a tintype picture.)

Jacob Pettry, and therefore the aunt of Jacob William Pettry (the Mormon). So I married into a family with as many twists and turns as the Hurt family.

The presence of a doctor, and an entree to medical school, in the family probably accounts for the presence of several doctors in the next generation of this very rural family. Jacob Pettry had died in 1911, but, as I have said, Victoria was still alive when we were married in 1928. She actually lived until 1933, and for a while had a house near us on Drews Creek. She never actually lived there after we built our house, because she had gone to Dry Branch in Kanawha County to live with her daughter, Don's Aunt Mary Kittinger, after she broke her hip on our wedding day. I only met her a few times.

Mary Etta Hunter Jarrell, came from a locally prominent family of twelve children. Her paternal grandmother,

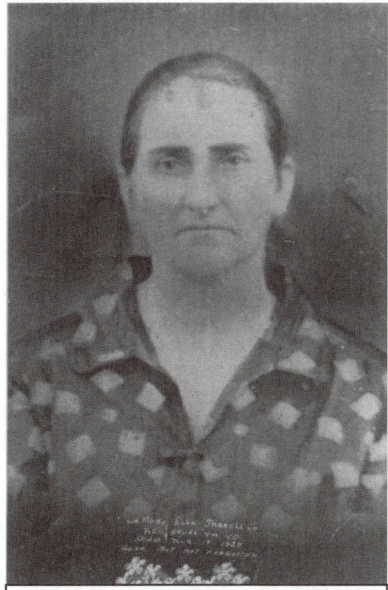

Mahala Pettry, was a first cousin of Jacob Pettry, so the cousin counting continues. Her father, Lewis Hunter, was a remarkable man with a reputation in the community not only as an important property owner, but also as a man of God and a community leader. He was a Union Civil War veteran, a farmer, a teacher, and served two terms as Deputy Sheriff and one term as Sheriff of Raleigh County.

Photograph 35 Mary Etta Hunter Jarrell

Lewis Hunter's wife,

Araminta Mandora Honaker, of Swiss descent, was the daughter of a Tazewell County, Virginia, farmer. She was a direct descendant of Henry Clay, not the great Kentucky statesman and orator, but his great-grandfather. One record shows that both Lewis and Araminta were born in Giles County, Virginia. The Lewis Hunter family was remarkable in that they had twelve children, and of the ten who survived to be adults, three became doctors, and one became a dentist.

We knew the Hunters quite well. Hubert Hunter was our dentist, and Robert Hunter was occasionally our doctor. Since Araminta died in 1917, I never met this remarkable woman. I only met Lewis Hunter a couple of times. He died in 1929, and I vaguely remember his funeral. It may have been around the time Phyllis was born, and I probably didn't go.

The accompanying photo of Araminta Hunter's funeral shows several people otherwise mentioned in this book. Among them are: Lewis Hunter, seated with hand on the coffin; their son Robert standing behind Lewis; their

Photograph 36 Lewis Hunter at the funeral of his wife Araminta Honaker Hunter (1917).

daughter Ida, seated beside Lewis; another daughter and Don's mother Mary Etta, seated beside Ida. Their brother, Charlie, is standing between Mary Etta and Ida, and another daughter, Minnie, is standing at the head of the coffin. Two of Don's siblings also are in the photo: Don's oldest brother Denny, standing behind and slightly to the right of Mary Etta, and his sister Minnie, partial face behind lady with hat in upper left. Other people are either unidentified or are neighbors.

One sad story that relates to this family was a diphtheria epidemic of 1875. The following may also have been a factor in three of the surviving boys becoming medical doctors. In late 1875, Lewis and Araminta Hunter had three children, James, age 4, Don's mother Mary Etta, age 2, and Annie, age 1. As Christmas approached, they were also expecting their fourth child, DeClifford who was born in February of the following year. Between December 14th and December 20th, James, and Annie died of diphtheria. Araminta's pregnancy must have made it even more difficult for her to cope with the loss of two of her children on the eve of Christmas. The events were so horrendous that Araminta was literally insane for some weeks, and we are told actually lived outdoors in a nearby wooded area, called Spring Hollow. This story becomes even more incredible when one considers the severity of winters in the mountains of West Virginia. Remarkable also is the fact that all of the other ten children born to this couple lived to be adults. *(At least one published record shows another daughter, Victoria, between James and Mary Etta, who also died in the diphtheria epidemic. However, a family journal from their younger brother, Dr. Robert Hunter, shows the birth and death of his two older siblings, but makes no mention of Victoria, so perhaps the one account confused two families.)* Some family records are given in the appendices.

Chapter Eight
Drews Creek

For about thirty years, we lived within a few hundred feet of one site on Drews Creek, a tributary of Peachtree Creek, which in turn emptied into Marsh Fork of Big Coal River in the western corner of Raleigh County, West Virginia. Drews Creek had carved out a "V" shaped valley, with little flat land except for its flood plain. Perhaps in the section of Drews Creek where we lived, the valley was shaped more like a "checkmark", with a steep slope on one side, and a long gentle slope on the other side at the confluence of Drews Creek and "Ma Kelly" Branch.

Photograph 37 Phyllis and Donald. This picture gives a glimpse of that little house Don built for us.

Through all of my years with my family, we had never owned our own home. When Don and his father, Samuel Jarrell, built that first home on the flood plain of Drews Creek, they built it on land given to Don by his mother before she died. So when we moved in just after Christmas of 1930, I was living in the first home my family had owned. Within two years, we had a flood, which narrowly missed our home, and a devastating fire, which wiped us out.

The road lead to "The Flats", or officially called Naoma, about three miles away. Naoma was a rather large plateau some 200 feet above the Marsh Fork of Big Coal River. The road through Naoma was a paved two-lane highway, while the road to Peachtree Creek, and ultimately to Drews Creek was an unpaved dirt road. The "Peachtree" road followed the river, although most of the way it had been cut into the hillside well above the river.

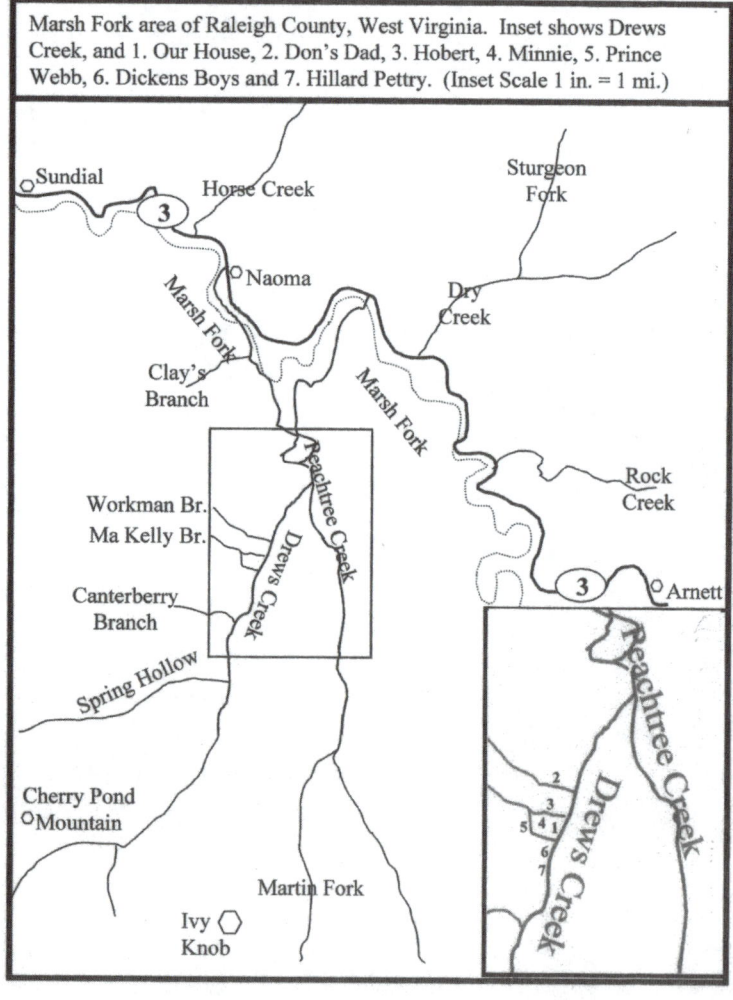

Marsh Fork area of Raleigh County, West Virginia. Inset shows Drews Creek, and 1. Our House, 2. Don's Dad, 3. Hobert, 4. Minnie, 5. Prince Webb, 6. Dickens Boys and 7. Hillard Pettry. (Inset Scale 1 in. = 1 mi.)

In fact, for about two of the three miles, the road was

relatively flat, but elevated about 200 feet above the river. This feature placed a steep hill at either end of the relatively flat stretch. These hills were natural roadblocks in the winter when they were snow-covered. So long as the road was blocked, we were practically marooned, with no way for people to get to their employment, or for children to get to schools. It was not uncommon for someone with a truck to break open the road by simply driving the heavy vehicle over the road, plowing aside the deep snow, and putting deep ruts in what remained. These ruts then showed following motorists where the broken path was. This "road-breaking" was perilous because of the steep drop-offs on the side of the road next to the river. Usually after a big snow, there would be one or two "casualty cars or trucks" abandoned along the road or over the side for a better day. To have broken the road was a status symbol, perhaps not unlike breaking a horse to the saddle. Much to my consternation, Don was always eager to be first to make an attempt at breaking the road.

Drews Creek generally flowed north toward Pineknob, where it emptied into Peachtree Creek, about a mile below us. About one-third mile downstream from us, or north, was Don's family home-place, where Samuel Jarrell, Don's father, lived. Don's sister, Ruby, and her husband, Kell Hendrix, lived with Samuel. Samuel was known in the community as "Coon", a name probably carried down from his hunting days as a youth. Mr. Jarrell was a carpenter and a farmer. He was known for his fiddle playing, and was reputed to have been pretty good at it, having played for square dances locally.

Although Don tolerated his father, it never seemed like he had the proper respect for his father, perhaps for some good reasons, not spoken of. He referred to him as the "Old Man", which in itself didn't prove disrespect, because in that society such reference was not out of the ordinary. There was never, or rarely, any sign of affection, and it was uncommon for Don to visit him, but, on the other hand, Grandpa Jarrell frequently dropped by our home, if only for a few minutes. He had a nickname for some of our children, which to them was a sign of, if not affection, at least recognition. They also remember him as being able to find things. If a coin or key was lost on the ground, he seemed to have a knack for finding it. This included four-leaf clovers, which all children loved to find, and he could point them out.

To our west, Don's younger brother, Hobert, owned a house, as did his older sister, Minnie Cox. Hobert married a few years after we did, so it was later on that he became our neighbor. Hobert was an automobile mechanic, so having him nearby was not without its benefits. Not only could he repair our vehicles, he also was a source of any tool imaginable, which we would borrow when the need arose. Don and Hobert were not only brothers, but also friends. However, like most brothers, they sometimes argued. Most of their arguments seemed to center about loaned, broken, or damaged tools, so there was a downside of having that friendly mechanic with all the tools living nearby.

Photograph 38 Pictured are Phyllis, Nell, Donald and Ruth. Minnie and I are barely visible on the proch.

Don's sister, Minnie, was a widow whose husband, Lindsey Cox, had been killed in the coal mines, leaving her with two girls, Ruth and Nell. Ruth told this story about her father's wake. She saw four angels who came in the door and retrieved his body, coffin and all. Later, she found out that these were hooded Ku Klux Klansmen, but the purpose of them taking the body is not understood. Although we knew little about the Ku Klux Klan, they were apparently fairly common in the area.

Our children were much younger than both Ruth and Nell, but they were among their closest relatives in terms of knowing what was going on in their lives, and seeing them often. Ruth was a bit wild, a real blonde party animal, but was regarded as a wonderfully good-natured person. Don loved to tease her, and on one occasion, she and her cousin (Don's sister, Dorothy's daughter, Ethel) had been involved in a ruckus at a local beer joint. When Don saw Ruth the following day, he had heard about the ruckus, and saw an opportunity to tease her. He said that there had been a ruckus at the beer joint and the police were looking for two girls. He said the first one was a pretty redhead, and Ruth asked about the other one. He said they didn't get a very good look at her, but they thought she was a homely blonde with a strawberry nose. At which point she knew he was making fun of her. If there was anything notable about Ruth, it was her looks. So Don's teasing only fit if you knew who he was aiming for. Nell was just as pretty, but the opposite in behavior.

Years later, Minnie became a devout Christian, but at this time, she too, had a bit of a shadow over her life. She had a live-in boy friend, Milt Hendrix, Kell's brother. There was a small bed in the living room, which the relatives were told was Milt's, leaving the impression that he slept there. We didn't know or want to know for sure, but it was a shadow, which may have haunted her for the rest of her life. Some years later, she too, had a mental breakdown,

93

and spent several months in the state mental hospital, from which she seemed to recover perfectly.

To the south of Hobert and Minnie was the Prince Webb place, and next to them was Jake Dickens' place. Jake was Prince's father-in-law. Prince was short in stature, perhaps five feet tall. Somehow, Don convinced Donald that when he got as tall as Prince, he could whip him. One could legitimately ask, "Why?" Prince was a nice easygoing fellow who definitely wasn't giving anyone any trouble, and the thought of a child confronting a grown man, regardless of size, is preposterous. In Donald's defense, one could speculate that he wanted to be prepared just in case. At any rate as people walked home from church, Donald would walk up close behind Prince so one of the other children could estimate whether he was as tall as Prince was yet.

Don frequently pulled stunts not unlike the "Prince Webb Affair", mostly harmless pranks on the kids. The neighborhood kids dearly loved him. He drove the school bus, so he was well-known by the high-school aged kids, and he knew them, and usually knew what was going on with them. When our girls started dating, he would pretend to have said something to the boy waiting at the door. One of his favorites, which he would have never said, was to claim to have told the boy "She won't be long, she only washes the part that stinks the most." He also claimed, although there is no independent confirmation, that he would watch until one of our sons polished their shoes, and then swap shoes with them. In his rendition of this story, he would then go out on his deputy sheriff rounds before they discovered what had happened. He also told a similar story about waiting for them to wash the car, and then taking it.

To the south of Jake Dickens, bordering the creek was a place owned by Jake's four bachelor brothers, Nev, Albert, Calvin and Tom Dickens. Interestingly, both Nev and Tom had lost a leg in accidents of youth. They joked, much to the astonishment of the children, that between them, they only needed one pair of shoes. These four brothers were collectively referred to as the "Dickens Boys" even by the children in the community. This became progressively more absurd as they reached old age. For a time, Tom ran a store there and was the postmaster.

Next to the Dickens Boys was the Hillard Pettry place, also on the creek. Hillard was a distant relative of Don's, although neither ever seemed to acknowledge it, yet they were good friends and good neighbors. Not acknowledging the Pettrys as relatives, perhaps was on purpose because it would give token recognition of the illicit relationship between Samuel Jarrell's parents Jacob Pettry, and Victoria Jarrell. Victoria, although not legally married to Jacob, lived with him and bore children by him while he also sired another family under the same roof by the former Jane Morris whom he had married in 1865. Since such living arrangements were viewed as immoral, it is understandable that it would not be spoken of openly by kinfolk. Jacob legally married Victoria in 1909 after Jane had died and two years before his own death. At that time several of their grandchildren were grown.

The Dickens Boys and Hillard Pettry were real farmers, who made a living off the land. Most of the others, including us, were part-time farmers who held down regular jobs. We rarely had problems with our neighbors; on the contrary, we borrowed from them and loaned to them and generally helped one another out when there was need. The Dickens Boys always had exotic produce of one kind or another. The favorites of the children were grapes and muskmelons. Muskmelons tasted like cantaloupes, but they were long, skinny, football-shaped with pointed ends.

Hillard Pettry would sometimes get in a bind with having hay on the ground before a threatening rain, and would prevail upon the neighbors to pitch in with to get the hay put away. Hillard's wife, Matilda, and daughter, Esta, were extraordinarily good cooks, so having lunch there during the workday pretty much paid for the labor. Hillard had a family of four sons and one daughter, so when the neighbors were there for lunch, it was like a church social. It was not uncommon for the ladies to have prepared two or three kinds of meats, beans, potatoes, salads and desserts.

Another wonderful event at Hillard's place was the making of molasses. This was a community event and all the neighbors found opportunity to stop by for a while to exchange gossip, and to sample the progressing goods. The children liked every step of the process from the raw sugar cane to the strappling and the final product. When we first moved there, Hillard operated a general store. However, his store was washed away in the flood of 1932, and it was never rebuilt.

Photograph 39 Don and me with the younger children in a swimming hole in Drew's creek.

Drews Creek was a tiny stream, with minnows, but otherwise no fish. The children would dam it up to create a swimming hole. A favorite spot was directly across the creek in front of our house. There was a huge flat rock, perhaps 25 feet long by 10 feet wide. They would build the dam across at the downstream end of the rock so that the rock itself provided a bank for the water to pile up against. At best, the water was never more than maybe two feet deep, but it was a worthy swimming hole for non-swimmers. There were crawdads and water snakes to see and the children fished for the minnows. In later years, they remembered that mostly they drowned earth-worms in their fishing efforts.

To somewhat complete the picture of Drews Creek, across the creek, the bank was a tree covered hill which extended as far as the eye could see both up and down stream, and rose very steeply to two or three hundred feet above the stream. This was of course, one wall of the "V" shaped valley. The children spent a lot of time in this hill, and no doubt learned a lot about nature, as there was not only abundant vegetation, but also considerable wildlife.

The Flood and the Fire: In July of 1932, Drews Creek, usually a tiny stream, became a memorable torrent. It had rained for several hours in the watershed at the head of the creek and in the area called Spring Hollow. When the combined runoff reached Drews Creek, it was more than its banks could hold. I remember Don, sort of playing, pushing things into the rising stream, with little concern, when water broke around him creating a tiny island where he was standing. When he realized what had happened, he was just barely able to wade through the new stream to get to safety. Water came up near our house, but because it was located at a particularly wide spot in the stream-bed, the water never quite reached our house. However, we began to see automobiles, and homes, and parts of homes wash by, and realized that while we were spared, many other people were suffering extreme devastation. We heard

97

of one little girl being washed away, and saw in the paper some days later that her body had been found perhaps 50 miles downstream. We supposed her body had washed by our home without us knowing.

I wrote a letter home to my sister Vernice (and the family) to describe the flood. When Vernice went through Mom's papers after her death, she found the letter, and returned it to me. It read:

Munition, W.Va.
July 22, 1932

Dear Vernice;

I know you will think I was washed away in the flood providing you have heard about it, but I have been so busy all week that I haven't had time to write. We certainly did have an awful flood Satur-day. Hillard Pettry's store, barn, corn crib with three hundred bushels of corn washed away. Bert Dickens' house and Warner Miller's house washed away, and nearly every bodys (sic) gardens and corn fields either washed away or were ruined by land slides. Cars, garages, smoke houses, barns, (p.2) and I don't know what all washed away.

Everyone said Hillard Pettry's cement cellar was all that saved us and the Dickens boys. His cellar headed over, and he lost six hundred cans of fruit. We weren't damaged so much. Our wire fence in front nearly all washed away, and the water was clear up in our yard. We thought surely our house would go so we went up on the hill. Don and Kell staid (sic) down there ready to move our furniture out. Then the water started falling and we thought all danger was past but everyone told us since that that was the most critical time.

The saddest part of all was that Ezekiel Webb's little girl was drowned. Minnie had a (p.3) three-day old baby, and was wading out carrying the baby and the little girl while "Zeke" went out with the boys. Minnie fell and lost the girl and grabbed for her, but missed her and she went on out of sight. She was found a mile above St. Albans with both arms and legs broke, her neck broke, and both eyes gone, and a lot of her hair gone.

Both of King Webb's porches washed away and his house was filled with mud. The creek runs under his house now. Barney Brown's house was (p.4) turned around and so was Rath Brown's store. Their gardens were all rock bars. I don't know what people will do this winter, or even now. The Red Cross is helping them. The road is all gone and they are letting the men up here build it. They pay a dollar a day. Don worked two days and is going to work as much more as he can. I know you wouldn't recognize this place up in here at all. There were so many land slides and so many houses turned around. Maudie Pettry's house was turned around and Doc Hendrix lost his kitchen. Big trees just kept coming down and pieces of barns etc. (Letter ends abruptly at bottom of p.4, likely additional pages were lost.)

A few months after the flood, my sister Faye was newly graduated from high school, and was persuaded to work as an unpaid or barely paid sitter for us. I was teaching at the one-room school at the head of Drews creek, and one of the neighbors, Virginia Miller, came to tell me our house had burned. She told me the children were all right, but I was in shock, and immediately went home. Going through my mind for the whole time was the little nursery rhyme:

> *Ladybug, ladybug, fly away home*
> *Your house is on fire*
> *And your children will burn*

That was one of those memories that never seem to fade. Faye was with the three children; Phyllis, Donald and Betty. Faye wrote to Vern to tell her about the incident, so I'll let her describe what happened in her own words.

Written by Faye Copeland, sometime between autumn 1932 and spring 1933

> *Dear Vernice;*
>
> *I suppose you know by this time about our bad luck. Don put a telephone call in to Ham Craig to tell you, and I suppose he did.*
>
> *This is how it happened----*
>
> *I was sitting in the dining room sewing. We had a fire in the front room too and Phyllis and Donald just had gone in there. Phyllis said "Oh Faye, look what Donald's done to the curtains." I jumped up and before I got in there to the curtains the flame had reached the ceiling and was making a wide sweep across above our heads. I carried Betty to the kitchen, opened the kitchen door and put Donald and Phyllis out then shut it and tried to pour water on the fire and throw blankets up against the ceiling, but it was too far gone and I knew if I tried to get anything out, Phyllis and Donald would run in after me. By*

the time I got in where Betty was the smoke (p.2) was so dense I couldn't see ahead of me I had to feel for the kitchen door. I ran up to the fence screaming "fire" hoping to get help from the Dickens boys but I had to cross two fences, help Phyllis and Donald over into the road, carry Betty and run up through the field almost to their house before they'd come out. Robert Workman, Calvin, Albert and Jake all ran out as fast as they could but they couldn't get a thing out. The only thing we saved was what we had on. I could have saved some clothes if I hadn't had the kids to look after, but the fire started in the room where we had our clothes, and I was afraid I'd lose one of the kids in the smoke. Minnie was even gone to B. Acord's that day.

We have been staying over at Ruby's since. Mr. Jarrell got some material and I made Phyl a dress and me one and Daisy and I have made underclothes – an underskirt apiece –for the kids (p.3) and a dress and a shirt for Donald. Ruth Cox got Donald a pair of Overalls. After the fire our wardrobe consists of :
Betty – the little tan dress trimmed in pink buttons and tape, an undershirt, diaper, and shoes and stockings.
Donald – his tan rompers trimmed in green, an underskirt, shoes and stockings.
Phyl – That blue dress and pants that were ordered for her, underskirt and shoes and stockings.
Don – his work clothes.
Daisy – that new dress I made for her and her underclothes, her jacket and that last winter's hat.
Me- that old threadbare dotted dress with the red and white ties, the worst underskirt I had, a brazziere (sic), bloomers, a pair of stockings and those oxfords that I got in August. The oxfords are the

*best thing I saved. Oh yes, and I happened to have
on that old black fur jacket that Bert made out of a
coat.*

*Several people have promised to work building a
new house, some have given Daisy material for (p.4)
the kids some dresses, two dresses for her and a pr
of pillow cases. Since all their toys were burned,
some of Daisy's pupils gave Phyllis a pretty doll,
Donald a ball and a little cart and a little cup and
saucer for Phyl.*

*If you and Bert have any underclothes or dresses – I
don't have a thing but a print I wish you'd send
them. Send that dinner set that the platter belonged
to, too I wish Papa could come over for a little while.
My two dollars, the one you gave me and the one
Don gave me later got burnt up. Daisy said for
Mama to write to Aunt Bert and ask her what she'd
take for her machine. She never uses it and Daisy
thought perhaps if she knew the circumstances she
might give it to her.*

*I've almost been down with a cold, the day of the fire
I took my jacket off to put over Betty and ran around
in the cold bare armed, but I'm glad to have a shel-
ter and Ruby and Mary have been (p.5) real nice to
us. Ruby has to go to the hospital soon but she is
able to walk and look after her baby.*

Hayden Eskens promised them a bed.

*Phyllis told me this morn if I'd have got her clothes
out she'd have carried the plates and rode out on her
tri sickle. She said, yesterday, she hoped we'd get
Papa out of the mail so he could build us a house.*

102

Donald set the curtain afire with a stick, Phyllis said.

There has been some debate over whether an eighteen-month-old child could even start a fire. I don't think the question of blame ever was discussed or even considered. Certainly a small child was not responsible in any case, and whether they were adequately supervised was far overshadowed by the fact that Faye took the appropriate action to save their lives.

After the Fire: After our house burned in 1932, we lived for a while with Don's father, and Ruby and Kell. It was

Photograph 40 This is the home of Samuel Jarrell where we lived after the 1932 fire. This is the opposite view of the house from what we would normally have seen. Our home would be in the distant background.

Photograph 41 Don's sister Ruby Jarrell Hendrix

crowded, and Ruby was expecting her first child, so this was not a pleasant time for us. However, I was introduced to the brand of country cooking that Don had grown up with, and I always felt that, because of Ruby, I became a much better cook. Don and his father were working as fast as possible on a new house for us. It was built a few hundred feet from the site of the one that had burned, but it was on a hill above the flood plain. That house on the hill was later added onto, and was to be our home until 1957, when we moved to Naoma, after all of the children had left home.

Ruby was the source of one of the sadder situations I have ever witnessed. Her son, Harold Guy, was born with an enlarged small intestine. His stomach protruded, and it was a constant problem for him to defecate. The condition was then untreatable, and, from early on, it was known he was not going to live very long; but Ruby

Photograph 42 Harold Guy Hendrix, c. 1938

refused to give in, and kept him going for about seven years with enemas, and just constant attention. When he finally died, she suffered a complete breakdown, requiring extended hospitalization. This also led to the breakup of her marriage to Kell.

It was so poignant that they started him to school, and had bought books and equipment for him, and very nice toys, all suggesting that they thought he would live to use them. I think this was my children's first experience with death, and Ruby's mourning was as near to unbearable as I have ever witnessed. It was like she somehow blamed herself, but we thought she had kept him alive far longer than anyone could have expected. After he died, there seemed to be much emphasis on the details of his death. Supposedly his last words were to Samuel Jarrell, saying "Come on Grandpa, go with me." Also, it was said that some of the feathers in his feather-pillow had formed in the shape of a crown or halo, which was taken as a sign that he had gone to Heaven.

When the new house was finished, probably spring or early summer 1933, we moved back and began to slowly accumulate furnishings to fill the house. Times were very hard, but we were blessed with many friends and relatives who had not only helped us build the house, but had also given us articles of clothing and furniture. None of the furniture was great, but we had two beds, one for Don and me and another for the three children. We had two chests for clothes, and one built-in closet in the front room, which we used to hang anything that needed to be hung up. We had four rooms in a square, two bedrooms, a front room, which would be a living room when it was furnished, and a kitchen/dining room. There was also a front porch that extended the length of the house and a small back porch off the kitchen. The well was at the location of the old house, about fifty yards from the front door and down the hill. There was a nice cold spring near our back door that probably was a factor in locating the house. We had a cellar, which was the only remnant of the old house left. This was a standard house; Samuel Jarrell must have used this plan several times before, because to my knowledge there was no written plan. Samuel Jarrell couldn't read or write, but he demonstrated that he was in many ways quite clever.

When Billie arrived early the next fall, it was crowded, and I was clearly overworked. That Mom would want to take one of the babies was both admirable and understandable. I suppose the fact that I let one of the babies go was practical and understandable, but I have often wondered how I brought myself to do that. I am sure others in the family have also wondered how I could rationalize letting Betty go for several months. Perhaps the stress of the house burning, living several months with relatives in a crowded house, moving into a new, barely furnished house, and giving birth to a new baby all within a few months had more of an effect on me than I realized at the time.

When Billie was a baby, probably around her first Christmas, we were coming back from somewhere and had picked up some candy and wrapped Christmas gifts for Gladys Kincaid, who was a child with some connection to the Charlie Stewart family. When we got to the John Jarrell Bridge that led to the old Peachtree road, it had been snowing and the bridge was slick. Don got out to check the bridge, and to walk me across because I was afraid of the bridge. For some reason, everyone except Betty was out of the car. For reasons still unknown, it went into reverse, and headed for the bank to go into the river. Don grabbed the front tire to cut the wheel, and made the car turn into the bank on the other side of the road. I was so scared that I set Billie down in the middle of the road. Of course, there were very few cars going by in those days. When our badly shaken family got back into the car, Gladys' candy and packages were spilled all over the back of the car.

There was always the problem of getting someone to stay with the children. We needed the income from my working, but we also needed someone to help with the housework, or, if the children were there, we needed someone home to look after them. In my memory, two such people stand out.

Hamie Brown was a middle-aged lady who lived up at the head of Drews Creek. Hamie was hired to do cleaning for me. She came in once a week to catch up on the laundry, and on the cleaning in general. I liked Hamie, and generally trusted her honesty; however, I suspected she was a bit of a gossip, and worried what the kids might say in front of her. Her daughter, Wavalene, came with her and played with Phyllis. I didn't particularly like that, because I thought it distracted Hamie from her work; but she had the same problem I had, she needed to have her child supervised. For what we paid her, I am sure she couldn't afford a sitter.

Don liked to tease her, calling her "Hamie, hamie, hame string". She got angry, or pretended to be angry, and retorted, "I'd rather be the hame string than the crupper that goes under the horse's tail."

Linnie Lee cleaned for us and lived in (after Hamie). There were Linnie Lee stories. Once, she had made supper, an otherwise unremarkable supper, except that it was piping hot. Jerry, being very hungry, was unhappy that it was so hot, said, "Linnie, can't you cook a little colder?" We had a poisonous antiseptic, bichloride of mercury that we used for serious wounds, like when one of the children stepped on a nail. Once, Lennie drank some of this antiseptic in an attempt to commit suicide. She lived, but we learned that the reason for the suicide attempt was she was pregnant and not married.

On one occasion, while I was teaching at Pineknob, Garnet was with a sitter at home. The sitter was doing some cleaning with lye. For some reason, Garnet drank some of the lye water, or perhaps she put some of the lye crystals in her mouth. The sitter came to the school to get me, and we immediately took Garnet to the doctor. The sitter had done something of a first aid nature; I am not sure what it was, but it must have been the right thing. The doctor said he thought there was some painful superficial burning of the throat, and that we would just have to wait to see if she healed. Within a few days, she was back to normal, apparently with no ill effects.

Don and I owned many different trucks and cars during our years together, and thinking of them brings many fond memories. We started married life with a roadster that Don had when we were dating. It had a rumble seat with room for two people, and we would often double-date with one of my sisters and her beau. At that time we also owned an old truck, though it wasn't very dependable, and needed repair. Later on, we usually had a pickup or small truck of some kind. One that served us well for many years was a 1941 model, ¾ ton Chevy.

Once Don had this truck loaded with hay, and allowed the kids to ride on top of the hay as he drove up the incline that led to our garage. Suddenly, the hay and children slid out of the back of the truck and gave everyone a good scare, but no one was injured! We still had it during the time the older children were in high school, and we used to let Donald drive it for their high school friends to load in the back and go to wiener roasts or other outings.

As mentioned before, Don drove a small bus to transport the miners to and from their work at Eunice. He kept the bus parked at home when not in use. It was small as busses go, and he called it "Short Dog." Our children were always fascinated by the bus, and were pleased when they could "hitch a ride" with the miners.

During, and at the end of, World War II, no new cars were being made. After the war ended and production resumed, people had to put their names on a waiting list to purchase a new car. Names were either drawn like a lottery, or they just went down the list in the order people signed up. Don became the envy of the neighborhood when he was one of the first ones to own a new car. It was a 1948 maroon Dodge Sedan. Donald and Phyllis were allowed to take the car several times to Concord College when they were students, and received many admiring glances from their fellow-students. Phyllis wrecked it around 1950 when she pulled out in front of a car at the intersection of Peachtree Creek and Route 3, at Naoma. The damage didn't look too bad on the outside, and we kept it from her until after we had sold it, that the frame was broken and the car was permanently weakened in the wreck.

In our later years, Don had a fondness for Pontiac cars, in addition to our usual pickup trucks. A few months before his death, he insisted on trading in our car for a new Pontiac so that I would "Have a reliable car to drive after I'm gone". I used this car until I gave up driving after I moved Florida.

We always had animals. Don always wanted to raise cattle for milk, as well as cattle, swine, and chickens to butcher so we had fresh meat. Since we didn't have refrigeration, Don and I learned how to cure bacon and ham, using Morton's Smoke Salt. We also canned beef, pork, and chicken in our old 7 quart pressure cooker. It took many hours of hard work to can the meat, but when we opened up a can of the meat or chicken, rolled the pieces in flour, and browned them in a skillet, we really had a delicious and easy-to-prepare meal. The children remember these canned meats as some of the best meat they have ever had. Of course, the canning was done on the old coal stove! Later Don also raised cattle to sell. We had an occasional workhorse to do the plowing for our garden, and for whatever other farming we did. When we didn't have a workhorse, we borrowed Don's dad's horse, Charley.

Two of the workhorses stand out in my memory. Dan was a large, dapple-gray, logging horse. He was a gentle horse, and the children rode him often. He was somewhat large for riding, and even with a saddle and stirrups they would usually need a boost to mount him. Dan had two habits that aggravated us to no end. First, he could jump practically any fence. By any, I mean we built fences that were seven or eight feet tall, and he could still get over them. While he never did this within sight, we surmised from the damage that he simply stood up on his hind legs over the fence, and brought his weight down on it. Under his massive weight, any fence we could build went from being several feet high to belly-high, at which point he would simply step over. His second fault was that every time he escaped, he made a beeline for his old home at the Ed Jarrell place at Dry Creek. Soon someone would recognize him as ours, and call us to retrieve him. In the two or three years we had him, this cycle must have occurred nearly a dozen times.

Once Dan pushed open the shed door, got into the grain barrel, and gorged himself on grain. He was miserably bloated, obviously sick, and we were afraid we would lose him. Don always seemed to know what to do in such a case, so he had me make some strong, hot coffee. He mixed it half and half with castor oil, and put it in an old wine bottle. He wrestled it into the horse's mouth, and made him swallow the whole thing. Needless to say, action soon began to take place, and Don announced, "Now he'll be ok." He was!

If Dan was large, our next horse, Deck was huge. He looked like one of the Anheuser-Busch Clydesdales. He was far too large to be used as a plow horse or ride, but Don got him at a bargain price from a logging operation that was closing down. He generally did what we wanted, but feeding him through the winter was somewhat of a problem. Another problem was that he was a kicker. He never kicked anyone, but liked to kick the side of the barn. In fact he virtually destroyed the old barn we wintered him in. Ultimately we sold him to another logging operation.

On one occasion, Donald and Jerry were taking Deck to the Cherry Pond Mountain to check on the condition of a farm that we had recently bought. As they were going up the

Spring Hollow, Donald was riding the horse, and Jerry was walking on the opposite side of the stream. Donald was riding along a path above the creek that was gradually becoming narrower. Finally the path got too narrow for Donald to turn the horse and was becoming too narrow for the horse to walk on. At that point, the horse slipped, and Donald jumped off just ahead of the falling-sliding horse. They both ended up in the creek bed, Donald none the worse for the adventure, but the horse was wedged feet-up, back down, in a huge pile of logs and saplings. The boys worked for about an hour to try to free him, in the process moving logs that weighed several hundred pounds. Finally, they gave up and walked home to get help, but mostly to get tools to work with. Don went back with them; I am sure he was not pleased at the thought of losing his fine horse. About half way up the Spring Hollow, they met Deck walking out. Somehow, he had freed himself, and appeared unscathed and even glad to see them.

There were lots of aggravations with all the animals, as well as the benefits we enjoyed from them. For example, every spring, we had to worry about the cattle getting into "stagger". This was the common name for death camas or, more often, camas (Zigadenys venenosus), one of the earliest plants to come up. It was very toxic to cattle, and could make them very sick or even kill them. It seemed to have a special attraction for them, and when they could get loose, they would make a beeline for the hills and the stagger. When the cattle got out, I would have to dispatch the children quickly to round them up before they found the "stagger patch". It seemed that this event was replayed several times each spring before we got past the "stagger season".

The cattle also made it hard to have flowers in the yard. I really didn't have much time to work with flowers anyway, but I enjoyed them, and made some attempts to have a few around the house. It seemed that every time I got flowers growing, the cattle would get loose and come right into the yard to trample the flowers. They also got into our garden a lot and destroyed some of the crop by knocking it down or eating it.

Once Don brought home a female beagle puppy that he had gotten from a family that lived on a mountain near the mine where he worked. We named the dog Billie, and she was to be a faithful mainstay for years. She seemed to have a brood of puppies annually, and we occasionally kept one. The rest we either gave away, or killed them in some way. She was a natural hunting dog, and would frequently hole a rabbit or groundhog. I don't think the boys caught much with her, but they dug a lot of holes.

Billie had learned to jump on the running board of the truck, and thereby go with the boys when they went any-where in the truck. On one occasion, the boys went to Edwight, about ten miles away, to pick up some freight. After that trip, Billie was no where to be seen. A few days later, Don saw her body by the highway near the high school, which was not far from Edwight. We surmised that she jumped on the running board on the dirt road at home and rode to Edwight with the boys, but was

Photograph 43 Billy, son of Billie, c. 1953.

unable to jump back on when they left because they were on a paved road, and likely started off too fast for her. We did have one of her male puppies, which looked like "old Billie", so we named it Billy.

A humorous incident involved a shepherd or collie dog we had named Shep. Dogs ran loose, and were not required to be on a leash like they are today; therefore dogs that "sucked eggs" were bad news. They would go into the barn and rob the hen's nests of the eggs we wanted for people. Such was the habit of Shep. After several days of "egg-robbery", it became clear that the dog would have to be destroyed or broken of this bad habit. Jerry came up with a clever plan. He got one of the eggs from the nest, pierced a hole in the shell, and filled it with a large amount of cayenne pepper. He then replaced it in the nest, and we all waited for the dog to "make his rounds". Pretty soon the dog bolted out of the barn, yelping and rolling in agony on the ground. He extended his tongue as far as possible, wiping it frantically on the dirt and grass, to try to get relief. We got a good laugh out of this, and the plan worked perfectly. He never visited the hen's nests again!

When Garnet was about four years old, she had a white nanny goat named Snowball. This goat was pleasant enough, but was nothing but trouble. It was always on top of something, the porch, banisters, truck, car, swing and always left it's calling card where it had been. She was known to eat freely from the garden and the flowers, and generally was a nuisance. On more than one occasion she likely was on the verge of a premature death. One such occasion was when she wandered on a freshly painted porch and proceeded to lie down, thus not only leaving hoof prints, but also gobs of white goat hair. On another occasion, she went through the screen door at Minnie's house and jumped on the table. She also followed the cows around, like she thought she was a cow. On these occa-sions, there were two things that saved her, first, there was no one to give or sell her to, and then there was Garnet to reckon with.

There was a gentleman who stopped by from time to time to see Don. He was known locally as Jim Greek, probably because he was a foreigner, not necessarily Greek. He bought and sold things, including animals, and had done business with Don several times before. On this day he bought a lovely white goat from Don. When the truck went by the school, as luck would have it, the children were out for recess. As the goat went by, she let out one of her signature "Baaaa" sounds, and, immediately Garnet knew what had happened. She tried to chase the truck down, but to no avail, it was too far ahead of her, and besides the paved road started just beyond the school. Needless to say, in some quarters it was sad at the Jarrell house that night, although most of us who had been doing the cleaning behind Snowball were glad to see her go.

There was one other animal story that needs to be told, if only for the lessons learned. Once Don brought home a bunch of small ducks. We perhaps had ten or fifteen. One of the lessons that Don learned pretty quickly was that ducks are not chickens. We always had chickens around the garden, and rarely did they do any damage. Occasionally they would peck a tomato, or scratch up some seed corn, but they didn't seem to be smart enough to go down a row digging up the seed corn. Crows were alleged to do that from time to time. Ducks on the other hand, as Don put it, "They don't just dig up the seed corn, they shovel it up!" They had to be guarded or they seemingly would wipe out the entire crop. They too, had their supporters in the family. In particular, there was one small sickly runt who had survived despite the odds, and he was a favorite of the children.

On one occasion, Betty, Billie and Garnet decided to get the ducks drunk to see how they would act. The "goods" was evidence liquor, possibly moonshine that Don was holding for a trial that never came. The girls soaked bread in the booze and fed it to the ducks, who gobbled it up with enthusiasm. Needless to say, they became inebriated, and staggered when they walked, much to the delight of their tormentors. This is the second lesson learned from the ducks: they don't hold their booze well. All of the ducks got sick, and about half of them died.

We always had chickens, and I didn't like to kill them. Sometimes, I would send one of the children to Minnie's house with a chicken for her to kill. She would wring its neck, a procedure that was abhorrent to me, because the head always tried to twist in my hand. If I had to, I would kill them by decapitating them with a hatchet. This seemed more humane to me since it was faster. We would then dip the chicken in boiling water so we could pluck its feathers. The smell of the feathers stuck with you for a while, and cutting up the chicken was also not my favorite thing. However, the fried chicken was delicious, and enough to make you forget the process.

We also kept hogs and cattle, and sold and butchered them. Don would lure the animal to be slaughtered to a spot where they could be hung up by spreading a path of kernels of corn. Then he would shoot the animal between the eyes at close range. I suspect this method was about as humane as possible, with probably little or no suffering. Anyhow, I would cringe listening for the pigs to squeal and in my mind go through all the suffering the pigs went through. We always dreaded the "butchering days". I hated the smell of the hot water and scraping the pigs. Despite my dread, we always enjoyed the pork and it was not at all uncommon for the neighbors to share in the fresh meat.

Our garden was in a field called the "Bench", right by Minnie's house. This particular field was on a flat spot with about ten apple trees in an otherwise hilly area. Don always seemed to be able to raise a really good garden. His specialties were tomatoes, lettuce, corn and beans. He also grew hay in other fields to winter the cattle. He wasn't stingy in applying fertilizer and growing special crops to plow under to enrich the soil. We all disliked working in the garden, but we enjoyed the results.

We always tried to save apples into the winter. The children were taught about the old adage, "One bad apple in a barrel spoils the lot." Literally, it means that a rotten apple will cause those next to it to rot also. The idea was that if you saw a rotten apple, you should remove it. We would, of course, salvage the apple by cutting off the spoiled part, and use what was left. It was up to each of us to carefully remove the bad apples in order to make the supply last as long as possible. Years later, one of the girls joked one day that she never knew you could eat good apples until she went to a grocery store to buy apples. When her purchase included a spoiled apple, the cashier threw it away and told her to go get a good one.

One of Don's older brothers, Jim, ran a general store and post office at Pineknob. We did much of our shopping there until supermarkets came along. Most of what we bought there was on credit. Don would maintain an account (or we referred to it as a "store bill") there, which was paid off either on my payday, or on Don's payday, usually about once per month. It was customary for the merchant to give a treat when a customer paid off his account. This usually meant a small bag of mixed candy, so the children always looked forward to us paying our store bill as much as Jim did. Jim and his wife, Nannie, had a large family. The younger three or four matched up pretty well with our children, and they frequently socialized together. This was not always our choice because they

116

drank alcohol and smoked which we hoped our children didn't do. Of course, the younger children eventually did both despite our best efforts.

Don's older sister, Amy, and her husband, Avril Webb, had three children, Howard, Lillian, and Mary. There were signs and rumors of child abuse and spousal abuse. Probably there was at least some truth to the rumors, because she left him sometime around 1930. They divorced, and before long Amy had serious medical problems which culminated in a nervous breakdown, hospitalization, and eventually her untimely death.

Photograph 44 Don's sisters Amy and Minnie c. 1925.

Because the family blamed Avril Webb for Amy's problems, there was no, or practically no, contact with him or the children for several years. Meanwhile, Avril remarried and had two daughters. At the end of World War II, Howard came back from military service and resumed contact with the Jarrell family. Howard and Lillian stayed a while with their Grandpa Jarrell, but Grady Dickens and his wife had adopted Mary. Suddenly our children had the novelty of adult first cousins that they had never really known about.

Avril was apparently unhappy in his new life, and his adult offspring were now free to tell about their childhood. Although I don't remember them telling any tales of horror, apparently the cumulative weight of all this on Avril was too much, because suddenly, without obvious forewarning, he committed suicide by ingesting the poison strychnine. He had left a suicide letter. At his funeral I was requested

117

to read this letter over a public address system. The letter was about thirty handwritten pages that seemed to ramble on and on and would have been of scant comfort to anyone. I only know that reading that letter was one of the most difficult things I had ever done.

Ed. Note: The 1930 Census (taken by George W. Hendrix), 28 April 1930, shows Hobert, Garnet, Mary, Minnie Cox with daughters Ruth and Nell and Howard Webb all living with Samuel Jarrell. It also shows Bert and Vernice living with Don and Daisy, as well as a daughter P. Eugenia (age 1 1/12 years). Presumably this child was Phyllis Jean.

The children also had several cousins on the Copeland side, but they weren't nearly so close to them for two reasons. First, my children were older than Mom and Pop's other grandchildren, who were all younger than our fifth child, Jerry. Second, they never lived close together, and consequently saw each other infrequently. There were some close relationships, however. Jerry and Maurice Trimble, Vernice's oldest son, were close to the same age, and fast buddies when they were together. In the summer of 1945, Jerry and Maurice stayed for a couple of weeks at Mom and Pop's house, and according to Pop, were a handful for nine and ten year-olds.

Subsequently, my children formed close relationships with their Copeland cousins through the Copeland/Hurt reunion. Louise Fox, as well as Vernice's sons, Maurice and Mike Trimble, and Lowell's son, Steve, as well as Luke's son and daughters, are frequent participants. My children had less interaction with Warren and Faye's children, again because of the age difference and distance. Faye's children lived in Indiana, while Warren's lived in Florida.

When Don worked in the mines, he also ran a bill at the "company store." Each payday, he would bring home a case of Pepsi Cola, which we would split eight ways, three bottles each. He would also bring us each a whole pint of ice cream. What a treat this was and how we looked forward to our share of the ice cream. One of the reasons for running an account there was that you could use company script, or company issued currency. The reason the company issued script was to control employees spending, as script was only redeemable at company stores and gas stations. Other merchants would accept script, but at only a fraction of face value. Employees could "cut script" or get an advance on their pay before payday. For this favor by the company, employees were therefore coerced to trade at the company store. This is the origin of the Tennessee Ernie Ford song "I Owe My Soul to the Company Store." Don almost never "cut script", but he frequently would be in possession of script as a result of some trade or the repayment of a loan by one of his fellow employees.

Electricity came to Drews Creek around 1940. Before that, we used kerosene lamps and lanterns for lighting, and for refrigeration, we used a spring box in our spring at the back of the house. Hobert had taken courses in electricity at Beckley College (now Mountain State University) in order to qualify for work as an electrician in the coal mines and he occasionally did residential work as well, wiring neighbors' houses for electricity. He did the initial wiring for our house as well. He was careful with his work and insisted, for example, that armored cable was used where needed and that proper fuses were used to protect the circuits from overload. (Circuit breakers were not in use for residential work at that time.) While this first electrical work required extension at a later date, for example, to install wall outlets, it served our purposes quite well at that time. So, although a family member did the first electrical work for our home, it was installed properly, using safety code standards current at that time. It was a day to remember when the electricity was turned on.

When wires were being strung by the electric utility, on one occasion they were left "neck high" for children. Phyllis was coming back from Minnie's when it was nearly dark; a dog got after her. She nearly hung herself on the wire and was thrown back to the ground with "rope burns" on her neck. Needless to say, this was prior to the current era of runaway lawsuits. Betty had a similar story, but the offending wire was clothesline en route to Minnie's house. Betty thought she had been electrocuted. There was little knowledge about electricity, so the children were afraid of the electrical wires, whether energized or not.

When the lines were energized and light bulbs screwed in, the lights coming on was a miracle to behold. The children just couldn't believe that the lights could come on in an instant, and go off so it was dark before you got to the bed. We didn't do away with the kerosene lamps immediately because we just didn't trust this new electrical stuff. Our lack of faith was justified since we used them several times in that first year or so as the power service was frequently interrupted.

Donald remembers vividly "the wonder of seeing for the first time an electric light which, in my memory, was a bare bulb hanging from the ceiling,. Seeing the Delco-generator powered lights at Grandpa and Grandma Copeland's store at Hookersville somehow does not count in my mind, perhaps because it was not OUR light. Night seemed oppressive and impenetrable with the kerosene lamps, before we "got electricity," and the electric light seemed to carve out within the night a domain of brightness. The outside light seemed especially wonderful in this regard. I have almost no recall, however, of any details surrounding this event."

At first it was only lights, and people referred to getting electricity as "getting lights", and the electrical bill was the "light bill." We owned no appliances, and if we had, they would have been powered by running an extension cord to the light socket overhead. My first appliance was my pride and joy, a Montgomery Ward's refrigerator. By today's standards it was a primitive thing with a tiny icebox at the top, which could freeze ice cubes in aluminum trays. We could now keep milk fresh, and there were lots of things that we could keep on hand without fear of spoilage. The children loved warm milk, but this cold milk was really something special. Small containers of ice cream could now be brought home and kept for a while, although I never remember it lasting in our house long enough to make much difference.

I think as proud as I was of my new refrigerator, Don was even more proud of his new radio. Up to this time we had a battery-powered Stromberg-Carlson floor model radio on which the reception was extremely poor. I suspect we could only get a couple of stations. Then we got a new large table model Zenith. We could get Cable Tabernacle Hour from Cincinnati and the Old-fashioned Revival Hour from California with Rev. Fuller. We also ordered free books and Christian reading from them. Now we began listening to radio drama. Favorites were "The Screeching Door", and "The Shadow".

We listened to the political speeches in the 1940 election campaign when Franklin D. Roosevelt defeated Wendell Willkie. Only about a year later did we hear about the beginning of the second World War, and the attack on Pearl Harbor. That Zenith kept us up on the war effort with such names as Edward R. Murrow, Walter Winchell and H. V. Kaltenborn. The Zenith also had several shortwave bands, and I remember the children being concerned because people who had shortwave radios were suspect as being spies. The refrigerator and radio weren't the only things that came with electricity. Before long, we had bought an electric iron and a wringer-model clothes washing machine. It was lucky we bought them when we did, because the war made things like that hard to come by.

In the late 1930's and early 1940's, few people had a telephone. There was a local crank phone system that several people in the community were on. This was a "party line", where each party had an individual ring, and you supposedly only answered when it was your ring. However, it was not uncommon for someone to answer just to tell you the intended party was not at home. It also was not uncommon to have several people listening in, that is, eavesdropping. Samuel Jarrell and Don's brother, Jim, were on this system. Jim also had a rotary phone that was capable of contacting the outside world because it had access to a telephone operator in Whitesville, in nearby Boone County. Calls came in to Jim's store for all of the neighbors and messages would be passed to the intended recipient, either to a close neighbor over the crank phone, or by the mail delivery person since Jim also ran the post office. In an emergency, one of Jim's family would drive to deliver the message. The crank phone system gradually died out in the late 1930's as parts became hard to get and maintenance became increasingly difficult.

We never were on the crank system. In the late 1940's, when Don became deputy sheriff, the county required Don to have a phone, and so we got our first phone and our first phone number, which we kept for the next forty years or so. The first arrangement was just a cut above the crank phone.

It was a ten-party line, which meant we could hear the phone ring for anyone in our party-line collection. Each party had a distinct ring; for example I think our ring was three short rings. Others were combinations of two or three long or short rings. Again, this meant you could pick up the phone and inform the caller about the whereabouts of a person who wasn't answering the phone, and you could also eavesdrop, something which frequently happened, even in our home. The next step was a four-party line, which only rang at the home of the intended target. You could still listen in, but you had no way of knowing that the phone was in use, unless you picked it up to make a call. The frustration here was that if someone left the phone off the hook, it was unusable for, not only them, but for the other party members also. Finally in the mid 1950's, we actually got our own private line. In these years, Don served as deputy sheriff and later as state road foreman, and he had a heavy load of business calls, generally competing with what he regarded as gossip traffic.

During these years, most of our neighbors did not have a phone, so we would take messages for them. We also would allow them to use the phone to make calls. We never forgot the years when we didn't have a phone, and the humility of asking to borrow a phone, or causing someone else the trouble of having to deliver a message. Most of the neighbors were unfamiliar with using the phone, so many times we would either instruct them or simply make the call for them. Many times this involved either good news or bad news to a relative. For example, Jerry had to call Lovella Webb in Ohio for her brother, Kermit, to inform her of the death of their Father, Prince Webb.

My brother, Warren, was in the army, and was at Schofield Barracks when the Japanese attacked nearby Pearl Harbor.

123

Later he told stories about his experiences there. One unforgettable story was about a woman getting shot by strafing Japanese aircraft. She was crossing the road, and continued to run for several yards after she was decapitated. Warren drew a parallel to a chicken that continued to flop around without its head. When he told about it, he almost laughed, as if he was overwhelmed just remembering it.

We worried about Warren all the time, and listened carefully to the news about places where he was. His letters were "V"-mail, small thin sheets of paper to cut down on weight. Also his letters were censored, and lines would be blocked out. Phyllis and I wrote to Warren, who spent much of the war in England. She remembered the gifts he sent her, specifically a coin bracelet from England.

We worried that Don would be drafted, but he was deferred because coal was essential to the war effort. I think he also was too old for the draft, because he was thirty-six at the beginning of the war, and I think the oldest draftee was thirty-five. I remember the rationing system during the war. Shoes, gasoline, tires, liquor, sugar, butter and meat were rationed. A certain quantity of each was allowed per family, or per person. We never had enough sugar or gasoline, and some of the kids were particularly hard on shoes. Betty, I remember as always having worn out shoes. Don was able to trade his liquor stamps for stamps to buy other things, and poor substitutes were available. For example, canvas shoes were available with artificial rubber soles. They were cold, and they didn't last long, but they were better than nothing.

Don frequently dealt with a man named Montague at the Company Store at Eunice. He would be able to help Don get things for our large family. Once Betty was out of shoes, and she said, "Well, maybe old Montague can help."

Oleomargarine, later just "margarine", came along as a butter substitute. It didn't taste badly, but it was too white, like Crisco, to look like butter, so they packaged a little packet of orange food-coloring powder that would be mixed with the margarine to make it look more like butter. There were no automobiles made during the war. Don had bought a new three-quarter ton, Chevrolet stake-bed truck in 1941, so that lasted us through the war.

Whenever we went anywhere as a family, all the children, except one, usually Phyllis, rode in the back of that truck. Most of our trips were to Nicholas County to visit Mom and Pop. The kids fondly remember these trips. Apparently, we had no idea what they were doing from the back of the truck as we were traveling along. Stories later revealed that they would yell things at people we passed, and on occasion would throw things. Donald was doubtlessly the ringleader of this conduct. We did go to Green Sulfur Springs to camp overnight and pick cherries. Perhaps we did this a couple of times, and would buy a whole tree, pick all we could from it, and come home facing all the work of pitting and canning our "booty". We also went to Winchester, Virginia, similarly to buy apples, but during the war years, travel was kept to a minimum.

Up until the mid-1940s, we depended on our spring (20 yards from our back porch) for water. We also had an outdoor toilet about 50 yards in the same direction. Around 1945, Don installed a pump in the cellar, and pumped water from the well into our kitchen. The well was located some hundred yards down a hill to the homestead where our house had burned. There was a single faucet at a newly installed sink in the kitchen. As primitive as this sounds, it was a huge improvement over carrying water from the spring in water buckets.

About a year or so later, Don bought a hot-water jacket for our coal-fired kitchen range. This was a hollow wall for the combustion chamber of the range through which water circulated to be heated. A tall holding tank was then located behind the range to hold the heated water. The system was gravity circulated, in that the heavier cold water would flow out through a pipe at the bottom of the tank, through the jacket, and then rise through another pipe back to the top of the tank. Cold water from the well was input into the bottom, and hot water was drawn from the top for use. Now we not only had water, we had hot water, well at least so long as the range was being used. Water was still available only in the kitchen. Baths were still taken in a galvanized tub by carrying hot and cold water from the kitchen to whatever room would be used for the bath.

Photograph 45 House on Drews Creek built after the fire, and remodeled in the late 1930s - early 1940's. Picture taken in 2002.

Until after World War II we always had an outdoor toilet. This was a "one-holer" wooden shack, built over a pit, within fifty yards or so of the house. The "toilet tissue" was commonly Sears-Roebuck catalogs, and newspaper. It was common for children in the country to get worms, not only pinworms, which they got, but also large, grey-colored worms that resembled earthworms, several inches long. Perhaps the diet, or the life style of going barefoot, and eating fruit off trees or vegetables directly out of the garden without benefit of washing, contributed to this problem. The common treatment was a

126

terrible tasting substance called Vermifuge Worm Medicine. I would then require them to defecate on the ground, so I could examine the stools for these stomach worms.

Don now set about to build a new bathroom on the back of the house. This room had a concrete floor, no heat, but had a shower. Within a year or so, a new bathroom was constructed complete with bathtub, lavatory and toilet. At about that time, we also got a new electric water heater. Albeit crudely, with about half of the twentieth century already gone, the Jarrell family had arrived there.

There were no fish in Drews Creek. People said there were none following the 1932 flood. They did make a comeback, however, around 1950. There were fish in Coal River, but the closest point was on the Marsh Fork, about two miles north. On one occasion, Albert and Calvin Dickens, together with their neighbor, Hillard Pettry's son Bobby, were going to go fishing and asked if the children would like to come with them. "Fishing" to the children meant using a pawpaw sapling as a pole and twine as line, attached to a store-bought fishhook, or perhaps, in a pinch, a bent straight pin. The hook would usually be baited with either an earthworm from the garden, or with a cricket or other crawling critter which might be found under a rock or piece of lumber. Catching a real fish was clearly a rare event, no matter whether there were ample fish or not. However the day was not a complete loss, because Phyllis, in her effort to make a long cast of her five foot line, managed to snag Bobby Pettry in the lip. Despite this unfortunate incident, these old gentlemen, and their neighbor, invited the children to go fishing several times.

One rather forgettable incident occurred in the swimming hole across from the house on Drews Creek. Betty, Billie, and Jerry were swimming there at the time, which must have been around 1940. Billie was close to Jerry in age, and was normally his protector. However on this occasion, Betty and Billie had conspired to "duck" him. He was very much afraid of having his head under water, and became convinced that they were going to drown him, possibly with some suggestions from them. They pushed his head under and had proceeded to hold him under for what was likely a few seconds, but may have seemed like minutes to him. At any rate, he panicked, and came up throwing rocks. One of those rocks was perfectly aimed at his "protector-turned-traitor's" mouth, and broke out Billie's upper two front teeth. These were permanent teeth newly provided by nature.

Bert was visiting, and Jerry was her favorite. Both Don and I were away at the time, and when we returned, needless to say, we were upset with him. He was punished severely, but the children always said if Bert hadn't argued his case, I might have killed him. This was a terrible thing to happen to Billie. We were told by our dentist that nothing should be done about the teeth until she was eleven or twelve, three or four years away, so she went into Junior High School with this rather unattractive smile. She has borne the cost and pain of otherwise unnecessary dental work all of her adult life because of this incident.

Bert sometimes spent some of her summers with us before she married (and sometimes after she divorced), and several humorous events surround her visits. One particular incident occurred because of her interfering with the children's discipline.

Donald was complaining about having to do some chores, a not too unusual occurrence. Bert, always the poet, said to him:

"Don't be a jelly fish,
And have some spine,
You do your work and I'll do mine.
Now can you add a line?"

To which Donald replied without missing a beat:

"Yes, you mind your business,
And I'll mind mine."

Other incidents involved her hair. Bert was the picture of
vanity. She worked hard on her appearance, and expected
it to be first rate. On one occasion she was adding some

blue tint to her "salt and pepper"
hair, when she got too much, and
her hair turned blue. Of course, it
had to stay that way until it grew
out. While I could say things to
comfort her, and make her feel like
it wasn't as bad as she thought, the
children would laugh and make
remarks that revealed how ridicu-
lous it really looked.

**Photograph 46 Bert
in her later years.**

On another occasion, she was
giving herself a home permanent,
and misread how to use the perm
neutralizer. She just burned her
hair to the degree that it was coming out by the handfuls.
This was another time when I could try to minimize the
horror of what I was seeing, but the children thought it was
funny, and the truth had to come out. Don was no help,
since he was bald; he had bald jokes to tell, and had been
waiting for a victim. She was barely able to retain enough
hair to cover most of the bald spots with judicious use of
combing and head scarves.

My youngest brother, Warren was only eight years older than our oldest child, Phyllis. He spent lots of time with us in the summer when he was out of school, and helped care for the children. Our children loved him, and looked forward to his visits, even though he was a big tease, and loved to play tricks on them. He and the kids spent a good deal of time in the woods where Warren showed them such plants as ginseng and yellow root. On one occasion, he dared and bribed them for a penny, to taste Indian turnip which is extremely hot. He assured them that it tasted good. When they tasted the turnip, and were jumping around in pain from the hot taste, he laughed and laughed.

When our neighbors, "the Dickens Boys" got old, it became obvious to the community that they would need help. By that time, Tom had long since died, and there were three of the original five brothers left, all in their seventies, with the oldest Nev, perhaps in his eighties. I undertook to see that they got one good meal each day. After I got home from teaching school, I would prepare our evening meal, including three plates for them, and the children would carry the plates up the road to them. The distance was probably about one half mile. It always seemed like carrying three plates on a tray was not only heavy, but also unwieldy, yet I never remember them

Photograph 47 Don at the Dickens' boys well. Few of us could pass this well without a drink. Their old house is in the background.

reporting any spillage. I would also include a quart of milk each day. The children would bring back the dishes, including the quart jar from the previous day, to be washed with our dishes, and then we would have our dinner. (Not infrequently, they would also bring back something from the Dickens Boys' farm or garden.) I don't remember the children grumbling about this chore as they usually did about their own chores. I think we all realized it was us, or nothing, and that without us, they wouldn't make it.

When they got to the point they could no longer farm, Don and I bought their property. Part of the purchase agreement was that we would build them a new house, and that they would be allowed to live out their lives there. Their old house was poorly insulated, and was nearly impossible to keep warm with their fireplace in the winter. The new house was small, but well insulated, and was heated by a "Warm Morning" heater, which was coal fired, and much less work and more efficient than their old wood burning fireplace.

Eventually, after Nev had died, they reached the point that providing meals was no longer enough to keep them going. At that time Don persuaded them to go to the Old Folks Home at Sweet Springs. They agreed, but it was with much sadness that they left their home and farm for the last time. While the Old Folks Home was a beautiful place and was clean and nice, it wasn't home, and they were never really satisfied there. Sweet Springs was about 100 miles away, and to our knowledge, we were their only visitors, and that was infrequent. When they died, they willed our children all their remaining money, I am sure as a reward for the years of carrying meals. Each child got a check for about $300, which was applied to college expenses. This caused some grumbling on the part of some of their relatives who had been "missing-in-action" during their years of need.

I have talked a good bit about the Dickens Boys because they were an important part of our lives. Nev (perhaps for Nelve) Dickens, was the eldest of the four brothers who lived as bachelors next door, about one-half mile away from us. Nev took the daily paper, the Charleston Daily Mail, which was delivered, to the house. He kept the old papers, so when our children knew him, he had stacks of newspapers several feet high. To a school child this represented reference material, and they would lament, "If only I could look through Nev's papers, I could find something to write about." In reality, newspapers are not good reference materials, because the story is neither complete, nor totally accurate on any one day in the newspaper. Newspapers develop the story as more and more facts become known over time.

Probably the most unforgettable thing about Nev was his study of the Bible. So far as we knew, he read two things, the newspaper, and the Bible. We saw no other reference books. Yet he had a wonderful grasp of geography and history. He also had an interpretation of Bible prophecy, which would rival scholarly professors of the day. He never trusted the Russians, because he believed they were the "Rosh" of the Bible, who will rise up against Israel in the end times. He also recognized the monumental significance of the creation of the State of Israel in 1948. He didn't talk much, but when you got him on the topic of the Bible, he had a lot to say. I am sure he was a very positive influence on our children.

It might be pointed out here that my children, as was true of the neighbor children, went barefoot from the first warm days of spring until the frost of fall. Only school and church, found reluctant shoes on their feet. The liberty of going barefoot was not without its peril. It was predictable that within the first day or so of this newfound liberty, would come the first "stumped" toe. The rest of civilization probably referred to this condition as a "stubbed toe", but not us. Smashing it against some immovable object, usually a rock, would injure the toe. It would bleed, and turn various shades of black and purple, eventually after some days, and a thick layer of skin from the front would become mostly detached, and have to be cut off. At that point, the cycle was set to begin again the next time the child was distracted as he or she approached another immovable object. This process repeated itself several times each summer, so most children had at least one stumped toe at any given time.

Other barefoot perils were broken glass and tin cans, but nothing compared in sheer terror with stepping on a nail. It seems that it was the policy of the repairmen in the family to leave whatever boards were left over from a project, right where they were removed. If these boards had a nail protruding up through them, then luck, or Murphy's Law, would leave the nail sticking up rather than down. Maybe looking for fishing worms or other suitable bait would cause an otherwise safe board to be overturned. It didn't matter; if there was such a board out there, my children could find it. We didn't seem to worry much about lockjaw; although we talked about it. We just got the "burning stuff" (bichloride of Mercury) and painted the wound, and they seemed to heal well enough.

I have talked a fair amount about neighbors, but not about friends. I suppose that is because they were one and the same. Outside of school, I was pretty much swamped with work. The children needed attention, the house and the garden needed attention, and there was the canning, butchering, and putting away the meat. So there wasn't much time for social interaction. Yet we called most of the families in the area our friends. People who come to mind are the John Vealey family, whose sons Aubrey and Hubert and their families were close friends. The Tolbert Workman family lived at the "head of the branch" behind Don's Dad, and also represented special friends. Farther down the road, the Milton Webb family lived. They were special in that several of the sons were educated, and were a positive influence on my children. Willie and Opha Bone's family was somewhat older than ours, but their younger children matched up well with ours. Opha taught for a short while with me, and we were special friends. All of these people were also active with us in the local church and school.

For many years we heated with open fireplaces using coal. Several of the children slept in one room. I remember once that Phyllis, as a small child, became terrified at seeing shadows of the room furnishings on the walls, flickering by the firelight. She imagined that bears were in the room until Don and I went to comfort her. Many years later, we went to Burnside heaters, and later "Warm Morning" heaters, both coal fired. After the war, we put a coal-fired furnace underneath the house. It was a huge improvement, but was never as successful as we hoped. I suspect Don didn't quite install it correctly.

Sometime in the mid-1940s, supermarkets came to our part of the world. The most convenient to us was about thirty miles away in the little town of Crab Orchard, near Beckley. It was called the Carolina Supermarket, we guessed because much of their produce came from North Carolina.

It was worthwhile to drive the thirty miles about once a month to buy groceries for our large family. This chore fell to Donald (with a driver's license at age 15), and Jerry (4 years younger). I would make an enormous list and give Donald what I estimated was enough cash to cover the bill, and they would go and return with a ¾ ton truck loaded with groceries. There were rarely any problems. This is indicative of the level of responsibility that we placed on our children, even at a young age. Don insisted on this, probably because he assumed responsibility from the time he held his first job at age eight.

One of the benefits of these trips was a chance acquaintance with the butcher at Carolina Super Market. He was a young man working his way through college and also running for a seat in the West Virginia Legislature. We all watched with some pride the career of that butcher turned politician, Robert C. Byrd, who went on to become one of the most powerful U.S. Senators in our country's history.

Mom's brother, my Uncle Jube, would visit once or twice a year. He expected to be housed and fed, and this represented one more burden that I didn't relish. He was nice enough, and had stories to tell the children, but he was a bit of a nuisance. He sold nursery stock by visiting the people in the community and taking orders, which were then filled by mail. Once I sent Phyllis and another girl home from school to get something I had forgotten, and they were very embarrassed when they walked in on Jube bathing. He said something like "hupp, hupp!" Largely because of his sales, we had lots of berries. Many of them grew along the creek, perhaps spread by the flood, so berry picking was something we all did.

Photograph 48 Uncle Jube.

We would take huge (5-gallon) buckets and dish pans, and would bring them back full of wine berries or blackberries. Wine berries are related to raspberries, but have a distinct fuzzy shell that opens up to expose the berry when it is still green. They were delightful to eat fresh with milk and sugar, but also made delicious jam and jelly. That we filled all the containers was the usual sign we were finished. The heat was particularly bad, especially in the canning process, since we were already tired from the picking, and the canning needed to be done that day or at least early the next day. I canned some for pies or eating directly as dessert, and made jams and jelly out of the rest. Although there were wine berries all along the creek bank, and black berries on our property or at the Dickens' Boys place, the big pickings were on the Hunter land in the Spring Hollow.

I remember sadly that once we were coming home from berry picking in the Spring Hollow, and saw Luther Miller's son lying in the road, killed when Luther dislodged a rock on the hill above him. The rock subsequently rolled down the hill and struck his son. In retrospect, Luther said he could have stopped the rock, but just didn't bother. I can still remember the pitiful sight of Luther kneeling over his lifeless body, weeping and praying for his recovery, rocking his body back and forth, begging God to spare his son. How upset we all were.

Snakes and berries were inextricably linked in the minds of my children. This is because when, and where we picked berries coincided with the habit of snakes sunning them-selves along the edge of low shrubs, such as berry bushes. There were stories each child told of picking berries down near the ground, and virtually touching a copperhead snake. It was always a copperhead, mostly because it made a better story if it was a poisonous snake, and besides the other common snakes, the black snake and the water snake, would generally "high tail it" if a person got too close. The usual scenario is that the bucket was dropped with whatever berries had been picked, and only if there were still a substantial amount of berries in the bucket, would any of us dare go back for it. My usual remedy for the snake was a hoe. I had found that I could kill the snake with a hoe without my risking getting too close. My usual method was to send the fastest runner for the hoe while I kept my eye on the snake. Copperheads were notorious for holding their position while coiled to strike, so they would usually patiently await the return of the hoe for their undoing.

One of the best snake tales involves not berries, but the water well. We had a dug well, as opposed to a drilled well. The well was about two to three feet in diameter, and had a wall of rock surrounding it. The rocks were usually flat sandstone, laid in interlocking layers much like bricks, to form a very sturdy wall. It was not uncommon for a small animal, typically a rabbit, to fall into the well with the usual result that the water begin to taste unusual, and that was a signal to uncover the well and retrieve whatever had died there. On this particular day, Don along with Donald and Jerry, assigned themselves to take care of this nasty little chore. The well cover consisted of a four foot square ring made up of railroad ties, covered with one foot boards, four boards in all. They removed the two inside boards, which provided ample space for a child to shinny down into the well to do the deed. The smallest would clearly have the easiest time, so Jerry was therefore selected.

Don decided that he could lower Jerry down the well by his ankle until he could reach a two-inch pipe that came out of the bank about four feet down. He could then swing down to the surface of the water five feet or so below that, and retrieve whatever was down there. While Jerry was being lowered in the well, and as his head dropped below the remaining cover boards, he spotted a copperhead snake, coiled in the corner, with every appearance of being ready to strike. He was either too smart or too scared to scream, which meant that his entire body, and much of Don's upper body passed within inches of the snake, thankfully without incident. Only after Don removed his arm was the story told.

Now they had a real dilemma, with this highly poisonous snake in a position that Jerry would have to pass on the way out. Don and Donald, never at a loss for creative solutions, decided to get a gun and surgically remove the snakes head. They got a 410-gauge shotgun (a small shotgun), and placed it almost against the snake's head to where the blast would go into the railroad tie. With one blast, the plan worked to perfection, and the dead snake fell down beside Jerry in the well. It was retrieved, along with a small stinky rabbit in the same operation. Needless to say, we didn't drink much water for a while.

The elementary school at Pineknob was the social center of the community. There we had school carnivals, pie socials, and an occasional movie. Most of the time when we lived at Drews Creek, I taught in that school. It is ironic to look back and remember that the Bible and Christianity were an important part of the daily school routine. The Bible would be read, and taught, and verses would be memorized. The Rock Creek (or Dry Creek) Presbyterian Church people came to school for religious services from time to time. Those visits helped the children to grow and become established in their relationship with God.

I felt like I always had to work at home on my teaching. I would have to come home and build a fire to heat the house after school when Don worked nights. The children always had chores to do. They sometimes wrote all the chores on pieces of paper and drew for them, dividing them as equally as possible. It seemed to work out well most of the time.

I remember most of the teachers I worked with at Pineknob, especially Vada Webb, who married and moved to Tennessee, Preston Pettry, whom the children thought was a rather poor teacher, of the "old school"; and Edith Griffith, who married Don's nephew, Eugene Jarrell. Edith and I had a close friendship.

I also was in charge of the lunch program at the school. We had a cook who brought in her own home-canned beans and other foods which she made into delicious meals. Her bean, and potato soups were special favorites of the children. One of the things I remember about those schools at Peachtree and Drews Creek was ramps. Ramps are a delicious member of the onion family that grow wild for a few weeks each spring. There was one thing you needed to know about ramps, they made your breath foul, even surpassing their cousin, garlic, in this regard. In fact, it has been said that you could tell from a mile away when a person had been eating ramps. This was only true if they were eaten raw. Cooked they were equally delicious, but without their undesirable side effect. If a child who had been eating ramps came to school, they likely would be asked to leave because their foul odor would be so offensive to everyone about them. This fact then suggested that all you had to do to get a short school holiday was to eat ramps. For this reason, eating ramps became a favorite springtime endeavor for reluctant students.

The school also provided a place for sports. There was a field that provided a usable area for softball, which later became an adult community baseball league. Our children always looked for places to ride sleds when it snowed. They rode in front of the house, but the hill at the school was ideal, with a crowd frequently gathered there. About one hundred yards up the hill behind the school, near the tree line, there was an eroded spot (a geological slump). The slump was referred to as the "white spot", and it was a test of bravery to go all the way to the white spot before launching the sled. Not many sleds made it all the way down to the flat area on the road-level without some sort of a mishap.

The children also played games at home. "Ante-Over" was played by throwing an object, a ball if available, over the house. If it was caught, then the catcher could bring it back to the throwing side, and win points by hitting someone with it. It was best to sneak back so you could get close before throwing the ball at someone. Of course "Tag", "Blind Man's Bluff" and "Hide 'n Seek" were also favorites.

For some reason, the children were afraid of the men in the Turner family who lived at the head of Drews Creek. I am sure the Turners knew this, and would act like they were going to hit the kids whenever they saw them on the road. The road was a conduit for local communications, since we didn't have a phone. People passing by would relate local news. Sometimes we inferred local news by the appearance of people passing by. I remember seeing Orville Mullins drive by, and I told Don that his face was red, and that I believed he was drunk. How wrong I was! His son had been murdered by another young man in the community, and when I had seen him, he was overcome with grief. There were others in the neighborhood who had less than a sterling reputation, and both the children and I were somewhat apprehensive when they were about, and drinking.

I was very active in the local church. Samuel Jarrell had given the land for the church with the provision that it be non-denominational, probably not wanting to exclude the Mormons, toward which he leaned. The church leaders were Sam and Ollie Dickens, Opha Bone, Myrlie Vealey and I. We rarely had a steady pastor, but did have an occasional preacher who would come in for a sermon or two, or to hold a week long revival. I usually taught Sunday School.

One of the favorite visiting-preachers was Jake Osborne. Jake was the son of Samuel Jarrell's half sister Martha Alice Pettry, and therefore Don's half first cousin. Jake also figures into another story when he was at our home and pressuring Don to make a commitment to Christ. He literally pushed Don to make him kneel down and pray, which he finally did, but we were sure it didn't take.

One of the visiting preachers ran off with a lady in the church. Since both were married this was a scandal of monumental proportion, but after a while, both returned to their original spouses, and all was seemingly back to normal.

Christmas was special, but usually there was not a huge emphasis on gifts, because we could not afford much. We made homemade decorations, and went out in the woods and cut a tree. Many times it was less than perfect, and I remember lots of struggles on Don's part to get the trees to stand up straight. We usually had gifts that included things like oranges, large green-paper-wrapped apples, coconuts, candy orange slices, homemade fudge, hard candy, and chocolate drops. We also had fireworks at Christmas, as well as July fourth. We usually had a Christmas play at church, and always Santa Claus was a part of the celebration. We made snow ice cream when it snowed, and homemade ice cream in a crank-type freezer when we could get ice.

A very difficult period in my life began when I fell on wet grass on the incline leading up to our house. I landed with most of my weight on my left elbow, and sustained a deep puncture wound. I treated it with the usual home remedies, such as salt solution, iodine, and bichloride of mercury, but each day it got worse. It was very painful, stiff, swollen and I had a very hard time keeping up with my school and home responsibilities. After a few days, infection set in, and I really became alarmed when red streaks began moving out from the site of the wound. I went to the doctor and, after several weeks of treatment, it slowly healed. I didn't have full use of the arm for a long time, and it still pained me for at least two years after it appeared to be healed.

The first of our children, Phyllis, was married June 16, 1951 to Ralph Aquino from Brooklyn, New York, whom she had met while they both attended Concord College. Ralph was from a Catholic family, and his family assumed that the couple would marry in the Catholic

Photograph 49 Phyllis and Ralph's wedding, June 16, 1951.

Church. Since Phyllis was a Protestant, this would have been possible only if she agreed to bring up any future children as Catholics. She was not willing to make such a promise, so it looked like the marriage was over before it even got started! After a few weeks of "stalemate", Ralph and his family, being nominal Catholics, agreed to drop

142

their insistence on this provision, and to have the wedding in a Protestant Church.

Phyllis was working at that time in Whitesville, and made arrangements to be married at the Whitesville Baptist Church. Ralph's parents, born in Italy, had come to the US as young adults, became citizens, married, and established a thriving construction business. Both Mr.

Photograph 50 Mr. & Mrs. Aquino with Phyllis and Ralph's children, Donald and Sara., c. 1957.

and Mrs. Aquino came from humble beginnings, as we did, but their customs and culture were quite different from ours. Since they came from a large city, and were rather well-to-do, we considered them to be worldly and refined. We thought of ourselves as rather primitive since we lived way back "in the sticks", and had just gotten indoor plumbing, electricity, and telephones a few years earlier. Actually, our families had a lot in common, but we didn't realize it until we got to know them better.

One of the major differences between the two families was in the use of alcohol. This showed up clearly at the wedding reception, which was held in our home on Drews Creek, following the ceremony. Don and I did not use or permit alcohol in any form in our home. Ralph's family, being typical Italians, served wine and beer with their meals, and alcoholic beverages were a normal part of celebrations, especially weddings. It was rumored that Ralph's brother and a friend who accompanied them from Brooklyn, both being very mischievous, "spiked" the punch, and our family didn't know anything about it until everyone had "consumed the evidence". Much to our dismay, some of our family and guests enjoyed it just fine. We learned a lot about understanding and tolerance from the Aquinos, and kept in touch with them with cards and occasional gifts. Ralph and Phyllis brought them to visit us once after we moved to Naoma, and we let Garnet go to NY with them once to visit his parents. Ralph had been in our home a lot during the time he and Phyllis dated, and we felt like we knew him pretty well, that we liked him, and approved of the marriage. However, we were afraid that the differences in religion and culture might be too much for the marriage to last. Over the years, Ralph became very dear to us, like one of our sons, and I was so thankful to be alive to see them celebrate their Golden Wedding anniversary in 2001.

It took me nearly 25 years to get my college degree. I took the required classes at several colleges over the years, in summer school and evening classes. These included one summer at Concord College with Phyllis when she was enrolled there, several classes at both Beckley College and Morris Harvey College in Charleston. I'm sure that it must have been difficult for Don and the children to have me away from home so much, but I never sensed any resentment on their part or that they felt neglected. I completed the requirements for a BS Degree in Education from Morris Harvey College, and graduated January 24, 1950. I accepted my diploma with a great sense of personal accomplishment and appreciation for Don and the children who had been so supportive all those years.

Chapter Nine
The Naoma Years

In 1957, Don and I sold our house at Drews Creek and bought a house and general store owned by Tom and Lilly Jarrell located at Naoma, or as it was commonly called then, "The Flats". It was on the main road, Route 3, and three miles from our home at Drews Creek.

Photograph 51 This is a photograph of Don and me at about the time we moved to Naoma.

Garnet, who was now in college, stayed out of school one year in order to help get the store started. I helped on Saturdays and did most of the paper work. We got a local high school graduate to work and help Don run the business for about 5 years. When she married we hired another young woman from the community.

After 15 years we sold the merchandise and rented the building to some neighbors, who lived across the road from us. During the time that we had the store Don worked as road foreman for our district and as deputy

Photograph 52 Don in the General Store.

sheriff. Finally, I retired in 1971, and he in 1972. I had taught in Raleigh County schools for 46 years. Both of us were tired of being tied down, and we had lost trust in humanity since so many people would not pay their store accounts.

The house had only two bedrooms and we found out quickly that we did not have enough room for our large family, especially on holidays. The house was designed in such a way that it was necessary to go through the two bedrooms in order to get to the bathroom. It was said that Tom and Lilly designed the house this way in order to keep an eye on their daughter, Pebble. We turned the attic into two upstairs bedrooms with a bathroom, and remodeled the kitchen, putting an access door to the downstairs bathroom so that it was no longer necessary to go through the bed-

Photograph 53 The house at Naoma on a beautiful winter day.

rooms. We later turned part of the basement into a small bedroom. This became a favorite room for Don and me.

In that basement bedroom, we also put a wood burning stove, a television and a telephone, and enjoyed the luxury of not having to make our beds as unexpected guests were never in this area. However, this also meant that wood needed to be gathered to burn in the stove. Some of the children and their families came on the weekends to get the wood in for us. This became an "every-weekend" affair in the fall and a lot of fun. I would cook a big breakfast (biscuits and gravy, fried potatoes, bacon or sausage, eggs, and fried apples) for everyone before they went out to gather wood. Curt borrowed a log splitter one weekend to split the wood. This proved to be such a labor saving device that Kyle built his own splitter that was used thereafter.

Along with the house and store, we also "inherited" Bud Cantley. He lived in a small shed in the back of the store lot, which probably at one time had been used as a chicken house. Everyone called him "Uncle Bud". He was probably not over 5 feet tall, stooped, and a little stocky in build. He was rather cantankerous, and Don enjoyed teasing him. I remember in particular one Halloween Don stooped down, knocking low on the door of Uncle Bud's shed. Bud hollered "What do you want?" Don said in a low, child-like voice, "Trick or treat". Bud came to the door, brandishing his cane, and said in a gruff voice, "I'll trick or treat you!" What a shock he had when he saw Don standing there.

Uncle Bud's cats were pesky, sleeping on my porch furniture and getting underfoot when you were walking. One night Don was walking down the sidewalk which connected the store building to the house. In the dim light he looked in front of him and saw what he thought was one of Uncle Bud's cats sitting on the sidewalk. Being aggravated with the cats, he decided to "Kick the cat over the store". He got a big run and kicked the "cat". The cat turned out to be a blowtorch which Don had left setting on the sidewalk. To quote Don, "his toes turned up like a sled runner". I am sure he must have broken some toes and his foot was black and blue for quite awhile. This did not endear the cats to Don.

Gradually it became difficult for Uncle Bud to care for himself. I cooked some of his meals and we carried them to him but this was not enough help to allow him to live alone. Finally, his niece came and got him and cared for him until his death. We missed Uncle Bud, as he truly was a kind and good soul.

When we moved to Naoma we had an old dog named Billy. Don had never given any of the pets much attention while we lived at Drews Creek. After moving away from his friends and relatives he said, "That old dog is my only friend" and became very attached to Billy. The dog was not very well liked by some of the neighbors, especially Mr. Satterfield who owned a furniture store across the road from our store. Each Sunday morning, Mr. Satterfield would dress up in his suit, and walk up and down the road in front of the store. Don referred to this as the "Parade". One Sunday old Billy went out, and cocked his leg and wet on Mr. Satterfield. I guess he thought Mr. Satterfield was a tree of some kind. Don pretended he did not see this happen although he found it to be very humorous and told the story over and over for years. Mr. Satterfield never mentioned this occurrence probably because it was such an embarrassment to him.

In about 1960, Mom and Pop moved to Crab Orchard, near Beckley, in Raleigh County. It is ironic that they moved to Raleigh County after all the years of Mom disliking Raleigh County. I would have liked to think that they moved

Photograph 54 Pop in his favorite chair at Crab Orchard.

to Raleigh County to be close to us, and that may have been a factor. Perhaps a more important reason was that Vernice and Farley had bought a KrispyCrème Donut shop in Crab Orchard, and they had moved there. They were instrumental in Mom and Pop relocating. As it happened, they closed or sold the shop after a few months, and Mom and

Pop continued to live there after Vernice and Farley left. I think they stayed as a practical matter because everyone else had left Nicholas County, and we were the only family members left in West Virginia, and so there was no thought of moving back.

Photograph 55 Picture from Garnet and Curt's wedding. Next to Garnet is Don's brother Jim's daughter, Lois Ann, who was maid-of-honor.

Garnet and Curtis were married in 1962 at our house in Naoma. They had planned to have a simple out-of-state wedding with two witnesses. Don's brother, Jim, died at the time they had planned to wed and Don, depressed over his death, said he could not bear the thoughts of his baby going off to Pearisburg, Virginia, to wed and offered our house for her wedding. Garnet told him that she simply did not have time for wedding preparations as she and Curt could not get time off from work. Don made all arrangements, including the wedding cake and punch, invited the guests and even got our nephew, George Smith, Jr., to officiate. I was not very happy with this decision, but everything went along very smoothly, and Don was quite proud of his accomplishment.

We liked Curtis very much. He fit right in with the family and proved to be a great help and a good friend to Don. He and Don would go "coon" hunting and fishing together. Garnet went with them sometimes, especially when they went squirrel hunting. One time when Curt, Garnet and

Don were returning from Hardy County squirrel hunting, Don got a bad case of indigestion. All they had was some warm 7-Up and Alka Seltzer. Don swallowed the Alka Seltzer and drank the 7-Up. As they traveled along, Don kept going "Buuurp!" very loudly and abruptly. Curt could hardly drive for laughing.

At Naoma, there were some neighborhood dogs that got in the garbage cans every night. Don hooked electrical wires to a metal slab on the ground, and to the garbage can separated by a rubber piece of conveyer belt. Then he connected the wires through the light switch at the back door. Curt and Garnet were there, and Curt was concerned because the children were small, and he was afraid they would get into it. Don assured him it was safe, and they sat down to wait for the dogs. After a while, one came by and jumped up on the can. Just then, Don flipped the switch. They said it looked like the dogs in a cartoon, with its legs straight out and ears standing straight up, eyes bugging out, and yelping to the top of its lungs. After several other dogs got the treatment, his "dog-in-the-trash" problem was solved.

Don bought some "coon" hounds for them to use in their hunting. He had long wanted a blue tick coon hound, so he ordered one and had him shipped to our home. We named him "Blue" or "Old Blue"? I never cared much for family pets, but I became quite fond of him and some of the other outdoor cats and dogs we owned at Naoma. Blue was

Photograph 56 Don's blue tic coon dogs, Sadie (l) and Blue(r).

Don's pride and joy, so he was eager to try him out as a coon hunter. The way the hunters used the dogs was to take them out at night, and let them loose in a likely spot. They would take off running through the woods barking, and when they found a coon, they would chase it up a tree, and then stand at the base of the tree, "baying" (a different bark) so that the hunters could go to the tree and kill the "treed" coon. On one of the first occasions when Don took Blue out, he took off into the woods barking, and then stopped. Don waited a long time and heard nothing, so he went looking for him. He found him lying down, and when he tried to get him to stand, Blue just kept lying down.

Don ended up carrying him all the way out of the woods back to the truck, and of course by this time, he felt that he had been thoroughly cheated out of the large sum he paid for his "prize coon hound". He took Blue to the vet, who told him that the dog had diabetes. He said that because of inbreeding, this breed of dog is very prone to diabetes. He told Don to keep Milky Way candy bars on hand, and just before went hunting to give Blue a Milky Way and he would be OK. It worked, and Ralph used this incident as an illustration of diabetes in his Biology classes for years.

Don and his dogs had several years of happy hunting together, but Don's health became worse, and he was gradually losing his fight with cancer, so their hunting days had to come to an end.

We had not sold all of the land we owned on Drews Creek, so every year we planted a garden at the old "Dickens Boy's place" and the "Braden Webb plot". One year, Curt was plowing the garden with the tractor, when Don decided he would burn the old corn stalks from the year before. Curt looked up from his plowing to find he was surrounded by fire. He escaped injury in spite of having to drive as fast as he could though the flames. Although very dangerous, we laughed for years over this incident.

We had help from the children and their families in planting the garden and generally there was more than enough for all of us to share in the bounty. One year we buried the cabbage in the ground with the stalks up and stored potatoes and some fruits in a "ground cellar". A ground cellar is a large hole in the ground in which vegetables or fruit are placed. This is then covered with plywood or tin with an insulated access area and finally topped with dirt. It was so good to go out in the winter and pull a head of cabbage out of the ground, or to get fruit and vegetables from the cellar. That year Phyllis and Ralph got some potatoes before they were placed in the cellar. Don said, within hearing of Donald Ray (Phyllis' son), "I guess we will have to bury the rest," meaning to put them into the ground cellar. Donald Ray thought he was doing that to get rid of them. He said, "Well, Grandpa, if you are going to do that, I think we could take a few more". Don got quite a kick out of that.

One year we raised pigs at Naoma. That fall, when they were butchered, Billie and Garnet came to help with the sausage and the putting away of the meat. The care of the animals and the processing of the meat-- in addition to the aroma of the pig pen-- turned out to be prohibitive to attempting that again.

In 1966, Pop died. He had dieted most of his adult life for diabetes, but doctors in those last days found no evidence of that disease. In fact, his problem was related to his liver, and he frequently was jaundiced. He was in such pain that we all felt like his going home to be with the Lord was the most merciful thing for him. We buried Pop at our family cemetery at Dry Creek. Clearly, we missed him dearly.

153

After Pop died, Mom came to live with Don and me for a while as she was unable to provide for herself. I was still teaching when she came, and caring for her made for a very difficult time. Bert was retired at this time, so Mom and she decided, after a few months that it would be better for Mom to live in Florida. We went several times to see her, usually with Curt and Garnet. It was never difficult to get Garnet's children to go, as Elesse had a particular love for the elderly, and was fascinated with her "old Grandma". Also, there was Cocoa Beach close by which was a definite plus.

In 1968, Warren died suddenly of an unexpected heart attack in Florida. We were devastated, partly because it brought our own mortality into focus. He was a guard at the Kennedy Space Flight Center in Florida, and had complained of episodes that he thought might be heart related. However, doctors told him there was no indication of heart attacks, and in fact his supervisor was hinting that the episodes were either fake or imaginary. Warren's death was the first among my siblings since Garland had died in 1910.

Don was diagnosed with prostate cancer in 1969. He was certain this was an immediate death sentence since he had such an strong fear of cancer. His brother, Jim, his mother and three sisters, Minnie, Mary, and Ruby, had died of cancer. Several other family members, such as nephews, had been diagnosed with cancer so it certainly appeared to "run in the family". On one trip to Florida to see Mom, Don had a lesion on his abdomen where a drainage tube had been inserted following his prostate surgery. This lesion refused to heal, although it had been several months following surgery. Don was convinced it was cancerous. He asked the physician if he could get in the water at the beach. He was told the saltwater might aid in the healing process and to enjoy the beach. Much to our surprise and pleasure, the place did heal up after being exposed to the saltwater. Don responded well to his cancer treatment and for several years was relatively "cancer free".

We bought some land above "The Flats" (the John Jarrell property at Dry Creek), and had a cabin and fishpond built. We furnished the cabin so the children and grandchildren could spend vacations or weekends there. We had the pond stocked with fish, and a small building put up so we could keep a boat and fishing equipment in it. Don and I would go fishing often. We really enjoyed it.

Photograph 57 Mom with Jerry's daughter Nancy at the "camp".

The grandchildren fished, swam in the pond, and rode in the boat when they visited in the summer time. We had several family gatherings there. Some of our happier times were spent at the little cabin and fishpond. In later years, after Don's death, people started breaking into the cabin and the pond needed a lot of care, so I sold it.

Up from the cabin and fishpond, we turned a large plot of ground into a cemetery. Don had it marked off into plots and we sold several of them. At the time we sold the cabin and pond we also sold the cemetery but kept twelve plots for our family. Pop was the first person to be buried there in 1966. Ten years later, Mom died in Florida, after a long illness. Her body was brought back to be buried in the cemetery at Dry Creek beside Pop. Don was buried there,

155

and more recently, Bertha was also buried there beside Mom and Pop.

Don loved to work in politics and was very good at it. His jobs as deputy sheriff and road foreman were political jobs, so it was necessary for both of us to work during elections. In addition, the children were placed at different polling places around the District to hand out campaign literature. My family had always voted Republican. I think the only time I have ever been disappointed in Pop was when Don asked him to vote for a Democratic candidate. Don's job depended that candidate's election, but Pop refused to vote for him, saying that he "Would never vote for a Democrat". I felt that since the Democratic Party represented the working class of people it made more sense that I support Don's party.

In one election, Don filed my name, unbeknown to me, to run as a candidate for the Democratic committeewoman for Marsh Fork District. I won the election easily. Examples of job duties of the committee were to fill political vacancies should they occur, to have fund raising events, to attend the state conventions, and to vote on the representatives to the national convention. The committee also elected the party chairman for the county and got the poll workers ready for the elections. I held this position for eight years, and enjoyed it very much. One of the honors that came with this position was being invited to President Lyndon Johnson's inauguration in 1968. We didn't go, but the invitation was a precious honor to me and to Don.

Don and I went twice to Northern Ontario, Canada, fishing with Garnet and Curt. On one occasion, Billie, her daughter Barbara and Roger (Curt's brother) went. We had a cabin with very rough accommodations. The fishing was always excellent; we got up early and fished for around six hours. We usually caught a large number of walleye and northern pike that had to be cleaned. This provided our evening meal on most occasions. "Bill", the man who ran the lodge where we stayed, generally provided us a moose roast. We were a little timid at first as we had never tasted moose, but found the meat to be delicious and really enjoyed having it. Our entertainment at the end of the day, consisted of listening to music over the loud speaker system at the lodge. This system was very rudimentary and the records played were from the 30's and 40's. Don and I especially enjoyed this music, although the others found it to be a laughing matter.

Barbara and Don played checkers some nights, and when Don won, Barbara got real upset with him. He was supposed to have let her win every time, but Don failed to realize this being the competitive person that he was.

A scary event happened one morning. Roger and Garnet were in one boat while Curt, Don, and I were in the boat in front of them. The weather was rough that morning as we went out. The waves from our boat caught the boat that Roger and Garnet were in, tipping it to one side. The tackle box fell into the lake. Don's glasses were in the tackle box that sank rapidly to the bottom. Luckily, neither Roger nor Garnet fell out of the boat.

Phyllis remembers her family "house-sitting" during one of these trips. They actually stayed in the cabin at the camp and occasionally checked on the house. Of course, the fishing and swimming at the cabin made that a notable vacation for the children. She described it as a treat for her family. However, there was one period of discomfort or dread during our absence. Phyllis said "We 'panicked' to hear on the radio of a West Virginia family that was killed instantly when the logs on a log truck in Canada came loose and smashed their car. After some hours of fear, we were greatly relieved to find out it wasn't our family."

One of the highlights of our life was the 50th wedding anniversary celebration in May of 1978, given by the children. A reception was held at the Lions Club in Whitesville. Around 175 friends and relatives attended our celebration. The children did a wonderful job with the food and decorations. Although Don had dreaded this event, he and I both thoroughly enjoyed the entire day. The gift from our children was money to be used on a trip and a framed tribute of what we meant to them. This tribute was one of my prized possessions. We used our money from the anniversary and flew, along with Curtis, Garnet, Elesse and Curt, to Monterey, California, to visit Jerry and his family. Don was in a lot of pain at this time as he had metastatic bone cancer, and was having a lot of shoulder pain. The trip, for the most part, was very enjoyable except for Don's discomfort and a major delay at the Chicago Airport.

In July of 1985, I went on a trip to the Holy Land with Phyllis and Ralph. I will never forget this trip. I was 79, the oldest member of the group. Phyllis and Ralph, along with the people from their church, and some people from the surrounding area of Chillicothe, were in the group. Phyllis and Ralph secured a place for me to go with them. It's hard to describe the feeling of walking in the places that Jesus trod, seeing where He lived and taught, where He was buried, where He died on the cross, and other happenings of his life here on earth. I could almost think I was transported back to the time He was bodily here on earth, because the places looked so much like our pictures of what it was like at that time. It's an experience I'll never forget.

The only regret was that Don was not able to go with me on this trip, as he was sick at this time. In a postcard dated

August 1, 1985, I wrote to Garnet and Don: "Hope Don is doing OK and not missing me too much. We're going to see the Dead Sea tomorrow and possibly the Sea of Galilee. I think we'll visit the city of Jericho also. I think we go by bus on to Jerusalem tomorrow. Anyway we're getting up quite early and are seeing quite a lot of things. Love you and miss you, Mom." While in the Holy Land, Phyllis, Ralph, and I rode a camel. Phyllis fell off her camel, but I managed to stay on mine. I was telling Garnet about this and she asked why I rode the camel. I told her "Just for the experience of it". She really got a big chuckle out of this and told me that this would look good on my resume.

Betty stayed with Don, (and I'm sure Billie and Garnet helped out also) and they were scared "nearly to death" when we tried to phone, and when we couldn't get through, we promised to call later. Because we couldn't get through, they assumed the worst. They imagined we had met with some misfortune. It was near the time of the cruise ship Achille Lauro incident when the disabled American, Leon Clinghoffer, was shot and pushed over-board. Don had not wanted us to go because of this. The tour leadership had changed our itinerary to lessen the danger.

In July of 1986, the children gave me an 80th Birthday party. All six of our children, and several of the grandchildren were there. This was unusual as they were now scattered across the country. This was the last celebration we had when we were all together before Don's death. That same year Faye died of colon cancer in Valparaiso, Indiana. It was not such a shock as when Warren had died, because we all saw it coming for several months, but it hurt nonetheless. The hardest part was the knowledge that she was suffering and in pain up to the end. Within a month, her husband Buck Hanna also died. Apparently he just lost

the will to live without her. They left a severely handicapped son, George, age 43 years, and we worried that he
might not be properly cared for, but his brother, Bill, took
him in, and by all accounts he is well cared for.

I really thought my heart would break in two when Don
died. After several years of battling cancer, he was almost
bedfast for the last year of his life, and was in and out of
the hospital the whole year, with frequent bouts of pneumonia. Finally, on March 24, 1987, he died. I know this
was the saddest day of my life. Don was my "burden-
bearer." Now, I no longer had Don, and from this, I
learned a new dependence on God, and that He is always
there to solve our problems and ease the pain. Don and I
attended and became members of the Baptist Church, at
Pettus, during the time we lived at Naoma. We developed
many close friends, which became our church family. We
always had good pastors at this church, especially Mel
Jamison. Mel officiated at Don's funeral service. This is
what Don would have wanted, as both Don and I had a lot
of respect for Mel, and felt he was a good Bible teacher.
Don was buried in the family cemetery near the pond.

I love to read the Bible and study the scriptures. My
favorites are the Psalms, especially the 23rd Psalm. Others
include:
John 3:16 Because it tells us how to be saved
John 14:2-3 Assures that a place is prepared for us
John 14:12-13 Our assurance of answered prayer
Romans 8:28 All things work together for good to those
who love the Lord.
Romans 8:38-39 Our eternal security
Philippians 4:13 I can do all things through Christ
1 Corinthians 10:13 God will not allow us to be tempted
above that which we can bear
1 Corinthians 11: 24-28 Observance of Lord's supper

The Ten Commandments
The Lord's Prayer
Proverbs 31:10-24 The virtuous woman (this was read at
Mom's funeral service and the description fit her so well)

I love the hymns especially, "Amazing Grace" and "How
Great Thou Art". I love the Christmas carols and patriotic
songs.

Some of the principles, rules of thumb or insights that I
have found useful during my years include:

1. Judge not that ye be not judged.
2. A good name is rather to be chosen than great riches
   and loving favor rather than silver and gold.
3. Do unto others, as you would have someone do unto
   you.
4. A stitch in time saves nine.
5. Don't think too highly of yourself.
6. Pride goeth before destruction and a haughty spirit
   before a fall.
7. Don't count your chickens before they hatch.
8. A bird in the hand is worth two in the bush.

After Don died, I decided to start a Flea Market in the now-
vacant store building beside our house. My children helped
to put up signs advertising for people to rent booths and
display their wares. This business venture did not prove to
be worthwhile. I have often felt that if Don were alive this
may have done well, as he would have known how to
advertise or had the business connections that I lacked.

I believe the happiest time in life was the time Don and I
had together after we both retired, especially after we sold
the store. We found time to enjoy some leisure time
activities such as watching baseball games, college basket-

ball, and football. As I have told you, Don was an avid fan of the Philadelphia Phillies, and I was equally avid about the Cincinnati Reds. We also had our favorites in football, the West Virginia Mountaineers, and in basketball, we liked the Kentucky Wildcats. This was neither constant, nor uniform, and in fact, we seemed often to choose opposing teams to root for. One picture that the children remember form those days is my listening to a static filled radio broadcast of my Reds, while Don was watching his Phillies, or something else on television.

We both enjoyed gardening. I planted a lot of flowers in the yard, much to Don's displeasure, as they were a nuisance to mow around. I used to do a lot of sewing when my girls were in school. After I retired I made several dresses for myself, sewed some for Garnet's children, and on one occasion I made a dress for each of my daughters as Christmas gifts. My favorite leisure-time activity was working crossword puzzles, cryptograms, jumbled words and other puzzles. I liked to make quilts and enjoyed some crafts. I like love stories, mysteries, and stories that teach a moral.

After retirement, I also enjoyed trying out new recipes and making some of the old favorites. One of my favorite recipes was for Sea Foam Candy, and it became a tradition for giving at Christmas Time. The recipe came from an old Rumford Cookbook and is as follows:

SEA FOAM CANDY
3 cups brown sugar
1 cup water
2 egg whites
1 tablespoon vinegar
1 teaspoon vanilla flavoring
2 cups English walnuts, coarsely chopped

162

Put brown sugar, vinegar and water in large sauce pan. Stir until it comes to a boil and sugar has all dissolved. Reduce heat to medium and continue boiling until hard ball forms when a small amount is put in cold water. Pour over very stiffly beaten egg whites, beating all the while. Beat until candy looks like it is beginning to hold its shape. Add vanilla and nuts. Put out by spoonfuls on wax paper to harden.

In March of 1993, Kelton (Betty's Husband), was terminally ill with a lung disorder. Garnet took me to their house to stay for a week. While I was there, a big snowstorm hit, about 12-15 inches of snow fell. During the snow storm, Kelton started having a very difficult time breathing. Both Betty and Kelton panicked, as the weather was so bad they were afraid they could not get help. Betty called 911, and they told her they would try to get there but it would probably be a while. I went in the room with Kelton and held his hand and prayed with him. He calmed down and began to breathe easily again. I am sure God intervened in comforting Kelton. Betty called the rescue squad back and told them it would not be necessary to come that night. Kelton died a few days after this.

164

Chapter Ten
The Florida Period

In February of 1994, Billie and Kyle had to come from their winter home in Florida to Princeton for an appointment with the surgeon who had performed surgery on Kyle the fall before. Billie called me to invite Betty and me to follow them back to Florida for a visit. Betty and I talked it over and decided to go. We traveled all the way to Florida with Billie in front and Kyle behind us. We were getting off Interstate 4 at Polk City, two miles from their home, when Billie started to pull out and stopped because she felt she didn't have time before an oncoming car approached. Betty, seeing her start, decided she had time and accelerated, only to run into the back of Billie's vehicle. Betty's car was badly damaged, but thankfully neither of the three of us was hurt. Her car was so damaged it couldn't be driven, and Billie's vehicle had a great deal of damage also. Since Betty had to get her car repaired before we could return home, she started arranging repairs right away. She couldn't leave until her car was repaired, so Jerry and Fay came from Miami and took me home with them for a visit. I spent about a week with them, and then returned to Billie's where we spent the rest of our time As they brought me home, we were able to stop by Titusville for a visit with Bert, who was in a convalescent home there. In all, we were in Florida about one month.

All the way to Florida Betty and I had remarked how much we disliked Florida, and how we would never live there, but a month really changed our minds. The evening before we were to leave going home, we started talking about how cheaply we could obtain a place in Polk City to spend the winters. Betty suggested that we check to see if we could go together to buy a place. I agreed, and we went out to look at a few places. One, in particular we really liked but

165

we were only able to see the outside. We left the next morning telling Billie that if she could find a place, we would buy it. I don't think either of us felt anything would come of our decision. About two weeks later, Billie called Betty saying she had found a place and needed some money to hold it until we could come to look at it. We talked it over, and sent the money to hold the place, purchased airline tickets, and in two weeks time we had not only bought a place, but with the help of many wonderful neighbors and friends, had cleaned the place up, made many repairs, replaced the guttering, and closed it up for the summer.

Betty and I returned home with Billie in their van since Kyle had left for home just after we arrived in Florida to buy the place. We had begun a new life, and for half of the year we lived at 264 Waterview Drive in Polk City, Florida. The other half of the year, Betty lived in Kentucky, while I still lived in West Virginia.

That fall, while at Naoma, I was in the process of washing clothes and while crawling backwards down the basement steps, my method of navigating the steps, I slipped, hitting my heel. The result was a cracked heel. I could not look after myself, so Billie came and got me and packed my clothes for Florida. I stayed with her and Kyle until we returned to Florida. Betty picked me up in Princeton, and we made another trip with Billie and Kyle to Florida on November 1, 1994. That winter was not very enjoyable. It was a big adjustment for both Betty and me. We were both getting used to living alone, and now we were sharing a home. On top of everything else, I was sick all winter. I knew something was wrong with me all winter, but I didn't know what was wrong. After the fall I had taken, and the way I had felt all winter, I didn't know how I could manage alone at Naoma when I went home. I discussed this with the children, and they made me realize I needed to get rid of my home, and move to Charleston where I would be near Garnet. Curt and Garnet had a ground floor apartment that would be available in June, and so we began the process of my move while I was still in Florida. Garnet and Curt began doing some things to get the apartment ready before I got home. We did not know at that time that I was facing colon surgery. I was so anxious about the move; this was by far the biggest change my life had taken since Don's death. How many times I wished he were there to help.

The apartment had four small rooms, and I was moving from a seven-room, two-bath brick home full of memories and treasures, which seemed impossible to fit into such a small space. My home at Naoma also had a basement which had served as an extra bedroom in the winter time for Don and me, a pantry year around, a storage area for home canned goods, storage space for two deep freezes and space for the laundry as well.

A part of my life would be gone when I moved, because I had a big garden every year. I had a strawberry patch, a rhubarb bed, and a large tame red and black raspberry patch. I always had tomatoes, green beans, corn, squash, cucumbers, potatoes, green onions, lettuce, kale, cauli-flower, broccoli, green peppers, banana peppers, and just about anything that could be grown in a West Virginia garden. I really wondered if I could leave it all. I also always had my flowerbeds all over the yard and I felt all of these things would have to be left behind.

I had to choose only one bedroom suite, so the others would have to be disposed of. I took my sewing machine, one desk, and my dining room furniture. I purchased a new couch that would make a bed for company. I also insisted that my refrigerator be moved. It was large, and after much difficulty, they did manage to get it into the apartment by removing the doors. For months, I would look for something and realize it must have been left behind. I did not get to make all the decisions about what was moved and what stayed. The girls had to decide for me, as I was feeling worse all the time. The Saturday I was moved into the apartment was two days before I had a colon resection surgery. On Sunday, Garnet took me to her house to prepare for a colonoscopy. On Monday morning, they did the colonoscopy and admitted me into the hospital for surgery. At 88-years young, I recovered remarkably fast from the surgery, went home to the apartment after five days, and my children took turns coming in to care for me. I began to feel like my old self again, and returned to my exercising routine. Curt would come and get me and take me to their house to exercise on his machine daily.

I returned to Florida that fall, and began quilting again. That year I finished four quilt tops that my good friend Melesse Given, Curt's mother, had started before her death in 1996. One day Garnet was discussing these quilt tops, and remarked that she could not understand Melesse leaving four of these incomplete as she was generally so organized, and rarely began a new project without completing the old. I looked at Garnet and remarked, "Well she sure would have made my life easier if she had!" Garnet got so amused over this, and stated that Melesse would have gotten a kick out of my making that remark. Those four quilt tops were for Garnet's children, Elesse and Curtis, and they refer to them as "Grandma Quilts" since one grandma started them and another finished them.

The next winter I thought I would start a cathedral window quilt. I had made one, but it had taken me about five years to complete it. Betty had a cutting board and cutting wheel, so she cut out all the squares for me, making it much easier to do. I decided I would give Billie the cathedral window quilt I had worked on for so long, because she didn't sew and all the other girls did. We, Betty and I, did some of the sewing by machine, but there still was so much work to do, pressing all the pieces, tacking corners, and then just the quilting. It was hard work but so rewarding. I finished that quilt during the summer at home and decided to give it to Phyllis. I determined then to make one for Betty and Garnet, and eventually did make one for each of my daughters by making one each of the next two years.

We had such good times in Florida. I got to spend time with Jerry, Fay, Tommy, and Agnes, Fay's mom, whom I hadn't been able to spend much time with in years past. Bert and Louise made many visits to our home, as did Lowell and Ruth. We visited with Bert the first year we were there, while she was in a convalescent home in Titusville.

I even got an opportunity to renew an old, old, friendship with Maynie (Morriston) Rector. She found out I was in Florida and contacted us. Since she lived quite close to Polk City, in DeLand, Billie and Betty took me to see her. We enjoyed a day with her, and she took us to lunch at a very nice restaurant. We initially had trouble finding her home, but a friendly policeman in DeLand drew a map for Billie, which showed the way right to her door. I really enjoyed visiting Maynie, and we had so much in common because she was a widow too. We visited her the next year, also and brought her to our home for a brief stay, and then took her home. She always attended the Nicholas County High School reunions, and had news of all our classmates. The next year we called to try to visit her and we couldn't get in touch with her at her house. I called a neighbor who watched after her and she told me Maynie was in a conva-

169

lescent home in DeLand. We found out the name of the home was Cloister and we went to see her there. When we checked up on her the next year, she had died. She was ninety-two years old at the time of her death. We were the same age and had gone to school together during the early years and again in high school.

Every year we had a different craft we worked on. One year we made potpourri dolls. Kyle cut out the bodies for us, Betty and Billie made the clothes and I was the hat maker. We had a lot of fun making them; they are still sitting around in various houses. Another year we decorated tee-shirts, and gave a lot of them away as gifts. Betty and I did a lot of quilting, which was after I finished making the cathedral window quilts mentioned earlier. My eyesight continued to get worse, and soon I could not participate in the crafts. I had macular degeneration, which prevented me from doing a lot of things I loved to do. I bought a machine to assist me in reading my Bible and daily devotions. With the help of the machine, I continued to work crossword puzzles, which was one of my favorite pastimes.

One year, we decided to have the Copeland-Hurt reunion at our house in Florida. Betty and Billie made the arrangements for it. We had it in March because we thought people might want to get away for the winter. The turnout was very good for the distance so many had to travel. A lot of family who lived in and near Florida got to attend who had not been to the earlier reunions. It was a lot of work, and most people wanted to continue to have it in or near Summersville, so we never tried it again.

Billie, Betty, and I attended the First Baptist Church in Polk City, and I really enjoyed the services there. On one occasion, after we had been attending the services there for quite a while, I stayed home Sunday morning because I didn't feel very well. As the girls were leaving church the preacher asked them where their sister was today. They told him I was their mother, and that he probably wouldn't be seeing me again. They said they weren't bringing me back any more because everyone thought I was their sister. The pastor became a close friend over the next year or so, and we all delighted in this incident over that time.

I would go to the Baptist church when in Florida and then when I went home to Charleston I would attend the Methodist church with Garnet and Curt, but the Pettus Baptist Church where Don and I were members always will be my church.

We did so many things in Florida that made the stay enjoyable. Jerry, Fay, Tommy and Agnes would visit and I so enjoyed their visits. On most of the holidays we would have a big dinner at our place because we had more room than most of the others in the park. There were several people in the park who knew Billie and Kyle from West Virginia, either through work or family connection. We enjoyed dinners with these people and working with them on crafts, and community projects comparable to the time when they helped repair and clean our home when we first bought it.

Bert and Louise and Lowell and Ruth, as well as people from the park, attended most of the dinners in years 1995-2000, and many times Jerry, Fay, Tommy and Agnes would be there. The winters would go so fast, and then I would return to my little apartment in Charleston for the summers. While there, I would get to visit with Curt and Garnet and their children, Phyllis and Ralph and their family, and sometimes Donald and Joanne.

Early in 1999, Jerry and Fay purchased a new home in Salinas, California where they planned to move after he retired. Jerry was retiring in January 2000, and they also wanted a house in Polk City to use during the winters. In October, Betty, Billie and Kyle came to Florida to try to find a place for Jerry and Fay to live. They found an empty lot which seemed suitable, and called Jerry in Miami to tell him about it. He had been trying for about four months to come to a reasonable deal on a house they had seen in the park, but because it involved a separation and potential divorce, the negotiations were going nowhere. The lot sounded like a way to get the house hunting going again, and Jerry talked to the seller over the phone and right away struck a deal. Meanwhile Betty, Billie and Kyle were looking at manufactured homes to put on the lot. Pretty soon, they came across one they thought Jerry and Fay might like. Upon hearing about this house, Jerry and Fay drove up to Polk City to see both the lot and the house, and were able buy the house. The home was to be delivered in November, after Betty, Billie, Kyle and I would be back in Florida, so we could oversee the placement of the home on the lot.

Betty and I got ready and left Charleston to meet Billie and Kyle in Princeton to journey to Florida together. When we arrived in Princeton, there was a note on the storm door telling us they were at the emergency room at the hospital. When we went to the hospital, we found out Kyle was critically ill. He was running a very high fever, and they didn't know what was causing it. Betty and I had to go to Florida by ourselves, because Kyle was supposed to be there to oversee the setup of Jerry's house on the lot, and Betty would have to do it in his place. We arrived OK, and the house was delivered on schedule. Except for a few minor glitches and the overhanging shadow of Kyle's medical problem, everything went well. The trip down and the few day's in Florida had been very stressful wondering what was going on with Kyle, and we were very fearful for his life. After intensive treatment such as ice baths to hold his temperature under control, and exotic antibiotics, he finally begin to mend and was sent home from the hospital to recuperate. However, he was still facing six weeks of daily shots. The final diagnosis was an infection in a heart valve, a condition that is at the very least life threatening. We considered it a miracle that he survived without permanent damage. Jerry and Fay moved into their home over the Thanksgiving weekend, and Billie and Kyle were able to make it for Christmas. What a wonderful, thankful and blessed Christmas season we had that year.

Jerry was to retire at the end of January 2000, and we were all going to a retirement dinner and ceremony, in Miami. A week before his retirement, Fay, Agnes and Tommy went to Miami to be there for the ceremony and we were to follow on the day of the Friday event. On Sunday before his retirement, we were getting ready to go out for our usual Sunday dinner. Betty and I were waiting to be picked up by Billie and Kyle. I got up to go to the door, and tripped on a chair and fell. I knew at once I had broken my hip. Betty told me to lie still and she called 911. Billie and Kyle arrived just before the paramedics, who confirmed my suspicion of a broken hip.

At the hospital, they did surgery on my hip that night, and after four days, sent me to a convalescent home for rehabilitation. Betty and Billie took me to the home on Thursday, and on Friday morning, they all left to go to Miami and Jerry's retirement. I felt so sad because I couldn't go, but insisted that they go. Don and Arlene Hare, (our friends from Mercer County, West Virginia) visited me and took care to be sure I had everything I needed. They just took over doing everything my children would have done for me. Jerry, Fay, Tommy, Agnes, Betty, Billie and Kyle all returned Saturday from Miami, and then they all took over seeing for my needs. I stayed six weeks in rehabilitation, and during this time I had many visitors. Jerry teamed up with Billie, and Betty teamed up with Fay to visit at least once per day while I was in rehab. Some of them came every day and Tommy or Agnes frequently came with them. I especially enjoyed Tommy's visits. He was always a ray of sunshine with that never-ending smile. Garnet and Curt came down, and stayed a week visiting me daily or more often. Plus, I had letters, cards and flowers from the others and many friends, and I had visits from neighbors and from people in the church. I couldn't possibly have felt neglected. I thrived on the rehab regimen, and I won the award for patient of the month while I was there.

Perhaps I should describe Tommy for those of you who might not know him. Tommy is my grandson, Jerry and Fay's son, and he has been severely handicapped with cerebral palsy from birth. He is permanently wheelchair bound, and cannot talk, feed, or dress himself. However, he is very sharp, has an incredible sense of humor, and is one of the happiest people I have ever known. He literally lights up a room with his presence. His smile and sense of humor were the reasons I enjoyed his visits so much. This was another special thing about these last years in Florida...I got a chance to be around him for extended periods.

While I was in rehab, Jerry told me he was concerned that if something should happen to me that my half of our house could get caught in probate, and limit Betty's options. He suggested that I sell my half of the house to Betty, with the understanding I could live there for the rest of my life. I agreed, and approached Betty on the subject. This couldn't have come at a better time for her because she was thinking in terms of living full time in Florida, and selling her

174

Kentucky home. In order to move her furniture, she would either have to add on to our home, or buy a new one. She decided to buy a new home in Florida.

I did not want to move to Florida, and after rehab, when I was able to go home, I asked my doctor if I would be able to go home to Charleston in the summer. He said that if I planned to go, I needed to get used to doing everything for myself. He also said I should listen to my daughters.

Another thing that happened while I was in rehab was the death of my sister, Bert. She died in February, in Alabama, and I, of course, was unable to attend her funeral. She

Photograph 58 Picture of the last five surviving siblings taken at the 1988 reunion. (L-R) Vernice, Luke, Bert, Lowell, and me.

was buried in our cemetery in West Virginia. This was the beginning of a year of sadness as my brother, Lowell, died in September, in Virginia, and my sister, Vernice, died a month later, in Indiana. We started the year with five siblings remaining of seven who had lived to adults, and ended the year with only Luke and myself remaining.

Betty had our doublewide moved off the lot, and replaced it with a new modular home. She had provided for me, but I still planned to divide my time between Florida and West

Virginia. This same year Garnet retired, and she and Curt sold their home in Charleston, and bought a beautiful lakefront home in Polk City. I didn't have anyone left in Charleston except Elesse, who would help me get to the grocery store, doctor's office etc. She would help me, but I felt like this was expecting too much of her. Additionally, the trips back and forth were getting to be really hard to make, it would take me several weeks to recover from each trip. After weighing everything, I decided to give up my apartment and move to Florida with Betty.

All of my family came to help me move. I gave away a lot of things, and moved what I could. Betty and I hired a van together to move her furniture from Kentucky, and mine from West Virginia. We moved in on my 94th birthday, July 9, 2000. It was a terrible job to get everything moved and put into place. Betty had most of it to do by herself, but she had help. The neighbors came in and helped a lot. Billie and Garnet were not in Florida at the time we moved, but they came down and stayed a week and helped us. We finally got everything straightened out, and got to enjoy our new home.

In January 2001, we bought a 24' pontoon party boat. Betty and I, Jerry and Fay, and Billie and Kyle each owned a third. We reasoned that since the community was on a lake, that we were missing out on the fun if we didn't have a boat. I think we all also wanted the boat to entertain our company, and perhaps, especially for Tommy. He could drive the boat, and as proud as he was at being able to drive the boat, I think we were all even prouder. He quickly became Cap'n Tom, and there are pictures to prove it. We actually bought the boat near the end of the first year of a three-year drought, so as it turned out our lake was then too shallow to launch the boat. However, Curt and Garnet had bought a similar boat, and we were able to store our boat on the shore at their home, and launch it readily into the lake adjacent to their property. We had wonderful times on the boat, although getting Tommy and me on the boat was a bit of a struggle for the heavy lifters. Later, Kyle solved this problem by building a floating ramp, and modifying the boat entry to facilitate loading wheelchairs.

All in all, my move to Florida was the best decision I could have made under the circumstances, and for my part, it was a decision I made myself. Although I loved my apartment in Charleston, I could never have had such wonderful fellowship and enjoyed my years as much as I did in Florida. No where else could I have had such close contact with my family. Garnet and Curt moving down was just the icing on the cake. Despite the distance, Phyllis and Ralph, Donald and Joanne, and most of the grandchildren made visits, some several visits.

I wrote the following words a few years ago. Now in looking back, I am overwhelmed at just how good and faithful God has been to me: "When I consider the future, I would be thankful if God lets me live to see the new century. I guess my next move will be when God sees fit to take me home to Heaven. I don't know if my being in the world has made any difference at all. I have tried to set a good example before my children and to instill in them good morals. I have tried to teach my pupils good morals as well as their subject matter, also to encourage them to go on to college. I have tried to encourage them to not leave God out of their lives."

Appendices

A: Children of L.L. and Nannie Hurt Copeland

B: Ancestors of L.L. Copeland

C: Ancestors of Nannie Hurt Copeland

D: Children of S.E. and Mary Etta Hunter Jarrell

E: Ancestors of S.E. Jarrell

F: Ancestors of Mary Etta Hunter Jarrell

G. Descendants of Don & Daisy Copeland Jarrell
     Part 1 Phyllis & Donald
     Part 2 Betty & Billie
     Part 3 Jerry & Garnet

Appendix A: Children of L.L. and Nannie Hurt Copeland

L.L. and Nannie Hurt Copeland

Bertha Ellen Copeland
1904 - 2000

(twin) Copeland
1906 - 1906

Daisy Dell Copeland
1906 - 2002

Vernice DeLora Copeland
1908 - 2000

Garland Winfield Copeland
1909 - 1910

Rita Faye Copeland
1911 - 1986

Lowell Ellis Copeland
1914 - 2000

Edwin Luther Copeland
1916 -

Robert Warren Copeland
1920 - 1968

Appendix B: Ancestors of L.L. Copeland

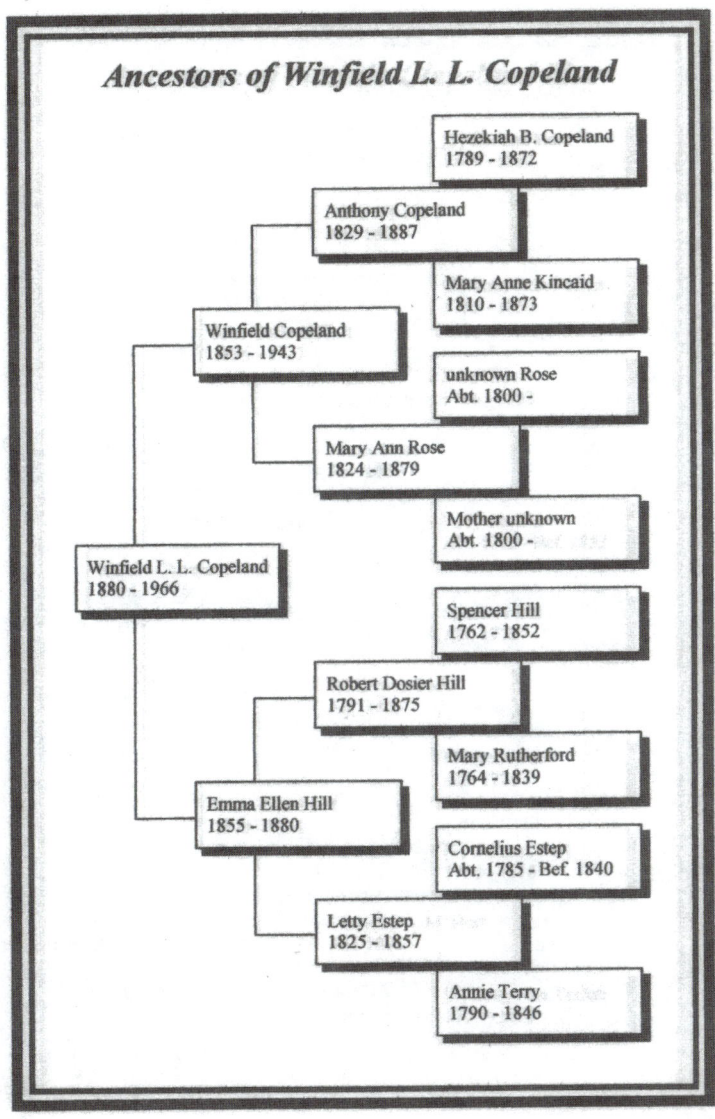

Ancestors of Winfield L. L. Copeland

Hezekiah B. Copeland
1789 - 1872

Anthony Copeland
1829 - 1887

Mary Anne Kincaid
1810 - 1873

Winfield Copeland
1853 - 1943

unknown Rose
Abt. 1800 -

Mary Ann Rose
1824 - 1879

Mother unknown
Abt. 1800 -

Winfield L. L. Copeland
1880 - 1966

Spencer Hill
1762 - 1852

Robert Dosier Hill
1791 - 1875

Mary Rutherford
1764 - 1839

Emma Ellen Hill
1855 - 1880

Cornelius Estep
Abt. 1785 - Bef. 1840

Letty Estep
1825 - 1857

Annie Terry
1790 - 1846

Appendix C: Ancestors of Nannie Hurt Copeland

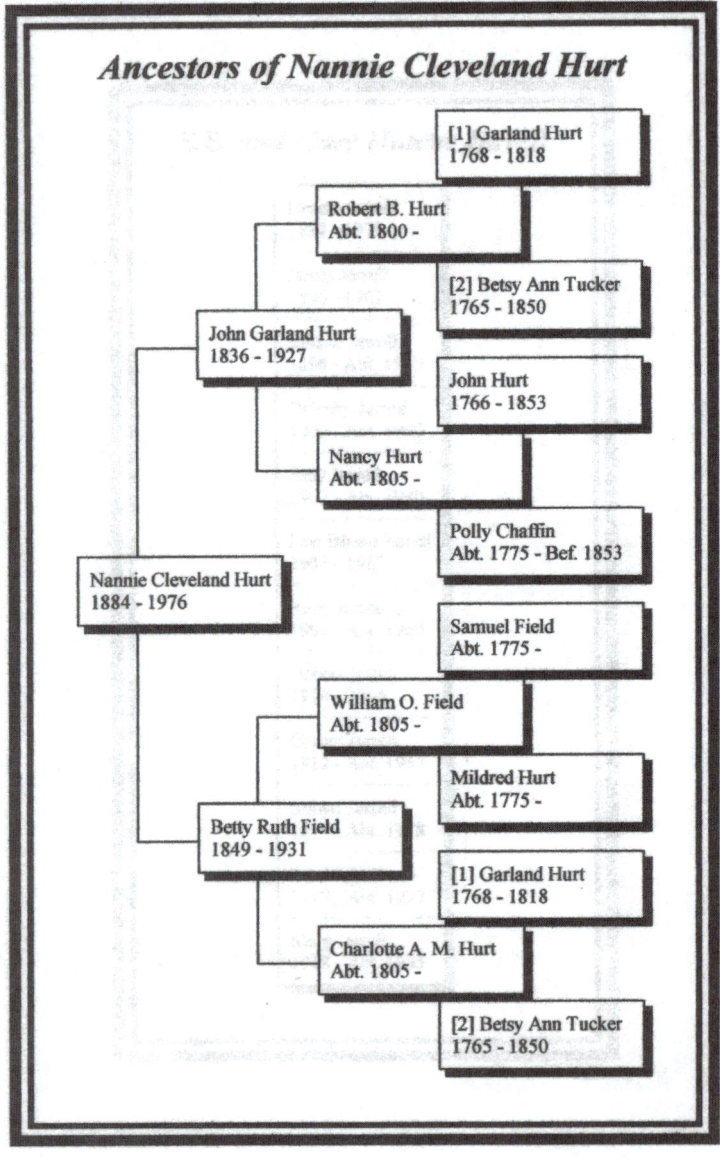

Ancestors of Nannie Cleveland Hurt

Nannie Cleveland Hurt
1884 - 1976

John Garland Hurt
1836 - 1927

Betty Ruth Field
1849 - 1931

Robert B. Hurt
Abt. 1800 -

Nancy Hurt
Abt. 1805 -

William O. Field
Abt. 1805 -

Charlotte A. M. Hurt
Abt. 1805 -

[1] Garland Hurt
1768 - 1818

[2] Betsy Ann Tucker
1765 - 1850

John Hurt
1766 - 1853

Polly Chaffin
Abt. 1775 - Bef. 1853

Samuel Field
Abt. 1775 -

Mildred Hurt
Abt. 1775 -

[1] Garland Hurt
1768 - 1818

[2] Betsy Ann Tucker
1765 - 1850

Appendix D: Children of S.E. and Mary Etta Hunter Jarrell

S.E. and Mary Hunter Jarrell

Dennie Jarrell
1894 - 1979

James Jarrell
1896 - 1962

Minnie Jarrell
1898 - Abt. 1960

Dorothy Jarrell
1900 - Abt. 1990

Amy Jarrell
1902 - Abt. 1930

Don Blaine Jarrell
1905 - 1987

Ruby Jarrell
1907 - Abt. 1960

Hobert Jarrell
1910 - 2003

Garnet Jarrell
1912 - Abt. 1935

Robert Jarrell
1914 - Abt. 1918

Byrd Jarrell
1917 - Abt. 1927

Mary Jarrell
1918 - Abt. 1985

Appendix E: Ancestors of S.E. Jarrell

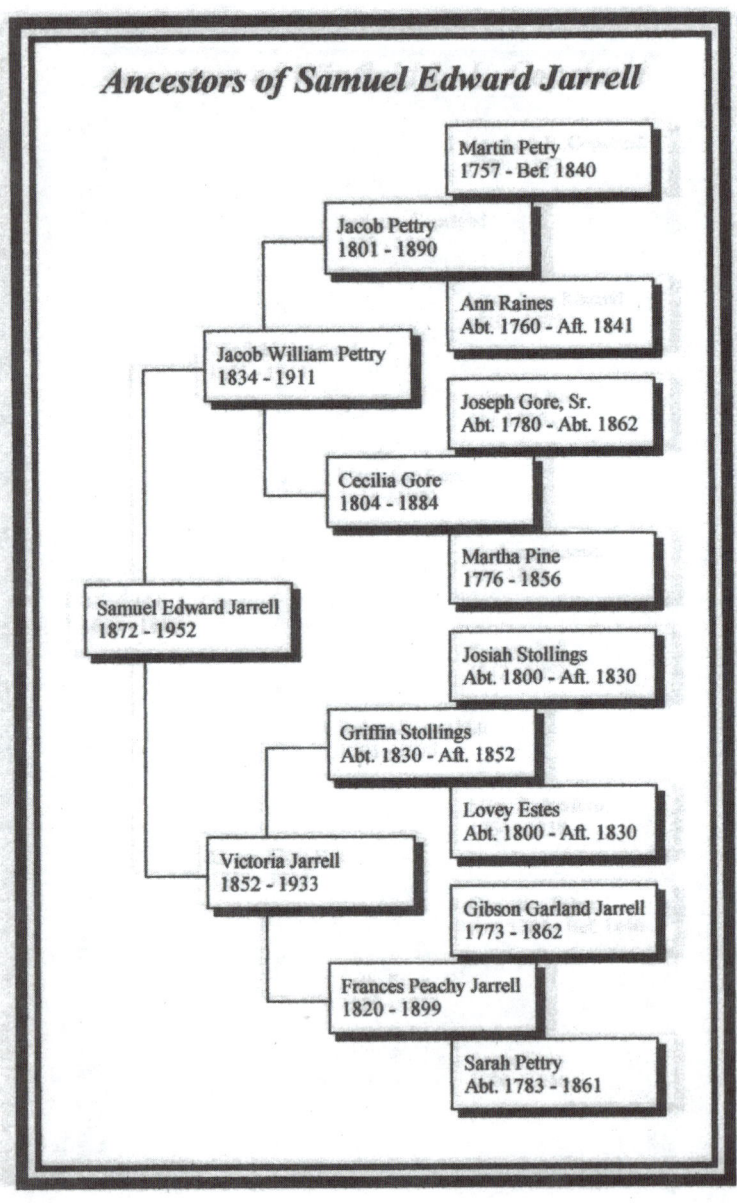

Ancestors of Samuel Edward Jarrell

- **Martin Petry** 1757 - Bef. 1840
  - **Jacob Pettry** 1801 - 1890
- **Ann Raines** Abt. 1760 - Aft. 1841
  - **Jacob William Pettry** 1834 - 1911
- **Joseph Gore, Sr.** Abt. 1780 - Abt. 1862
  - **Cecilia Gore** 1804 - 1884
- **Martha Pine** 1776 - 1856

Samuel Edward Jarrell 1872 - 1952

- **Josiah Stollings** Abt. 1800 - Aft. 1830
  - **Griffin Stollings** Abt. 1830 - Aft. 1852
- **Lovey Estes** Abt. 1800 - Aft. 1830
  - **Victoria Jarrell** 1852 - 1933
- **Gibson Garland Jarrell** 1773 - 1862
  - **Frances Peachy Jarrell** 1820 - 1899
- **Sarah Pettry** Abt. 1783 - 1861

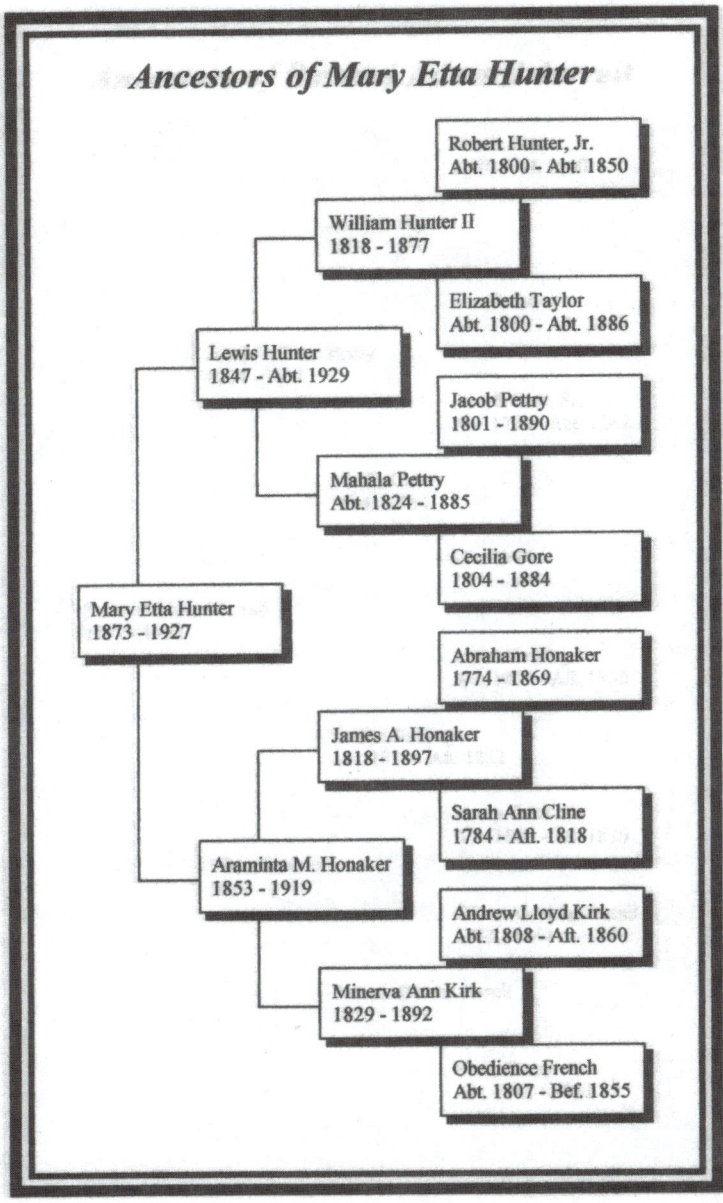

Ancestors of Mary Etta Hunter

Robert Hunter, Jr.
Abt. 1800 - Abt. 1850

William Hunter II
1818 - 1877

Elizabeth Taylor
Abt. 1800 - Abt. 1886

Lewis Hunter
1847 - Abt. 1929

Jacob Pettry
1801 - 1890

Mahala Pettry
Abt. 1824 - 1885

Cecilia Gore
1804 - 1884

Mary Etta Hunter
1873 - 1927

Abraham Honaker
1774 - 1869

James A. Honaker
1818 - 1897

Sarah Ann Cline
1784 - Aft. 1818

Araminta M. Honaker
1853 - 1919

Andrew Lloyd Kirk
Abt. 1808 - Aft. 1860

Minerva Ann Kirk
1829 - 1892

Obedience French
Abt. 1807 - Bef. 1855

Appendix G. Descendants of Don & Daisy Copeland Jarrell
Part 1 Phyllis & Donald

Descendant Tree for Ralph John & Phyllis Jean Jarrell Aquino

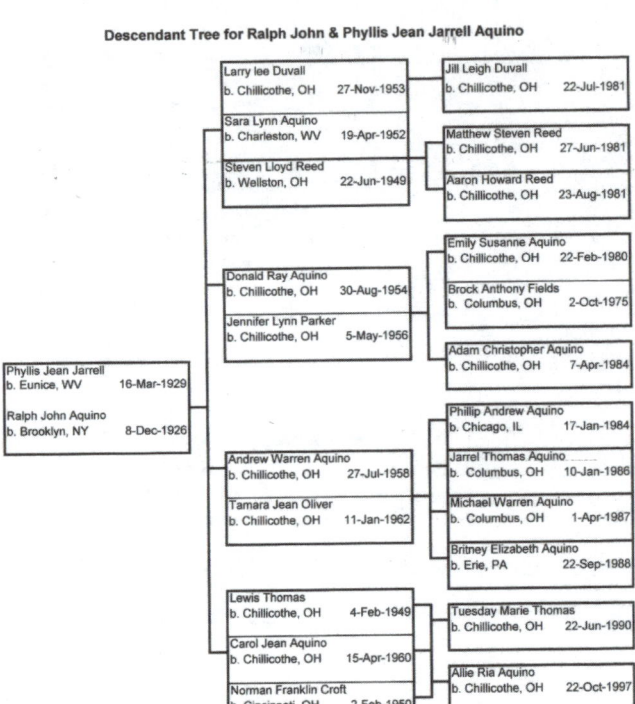

Descendant Tree for Donald Winfield & Joanne Lee Straley Jarrell

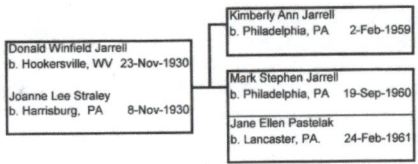

Appendix G. Descendants of Don & Daisy Copeland Jarrell
Part 2 Betty & Billie

Descendant Tree for Kelton Elbert & Betty Lois Jarrell Pennington

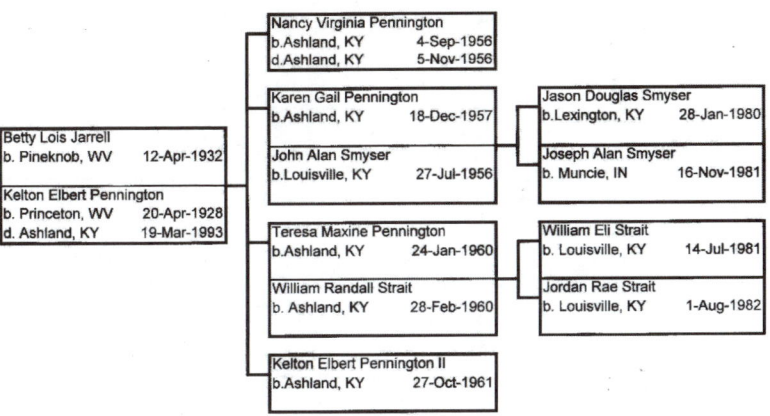

Descendant Tree for Kyle Preston & Billie Lou Jarrell Bailey

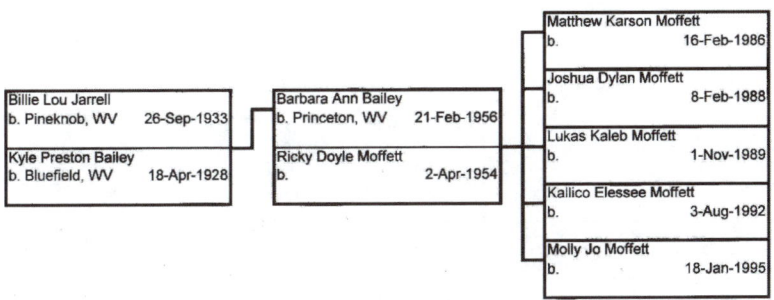

Appendix G. Descendants of Don & Daisy Copeland Jarrell
Part 3 Jerry & Garnet

Descendant Tree for Jerry Dean & Lois Fay Seacrist Jarrell

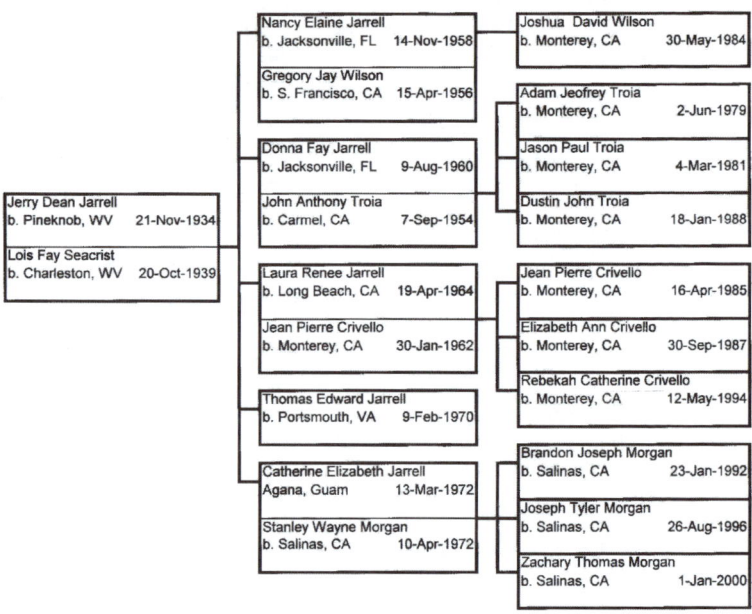

Descendant Tree for Curtis Alden & Garnet Elaine Jarrell Given

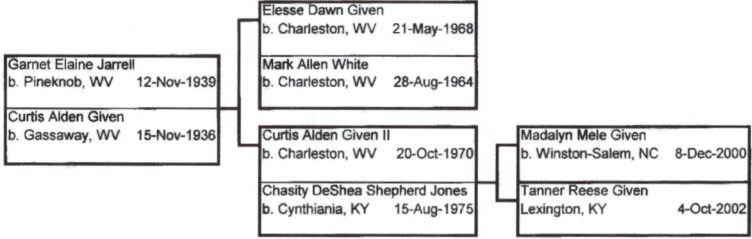